[YOU ARE PROBABLY **CLOSER** THAN YOU THINK]

JUSTIN AHRENS

LIFE

KERNING

Creative Ways to Fine Tune Your Perspective on Career & Life

WILEY

John Wiley & Sons, Inc.

LIBRARY OF CONGRESS CATALOGING-IN-PUBLICATION DATA:

AHRENS, JUSTIN, 1972–
LIFE KERNING : CREATIVE WAYS TO FINE TUNE YOUR PERSPECTIVE ON CAREER AND LIFE / JUSTIN AHRENS.—
1ST ED.
    P. CM.
ISBN 978-1-118-06782-6 (PBK.); ISBN 978-1-118-13907-3 (EBK); ISBN 978-1-118-13908-0 (EBK); ISBN 978-1-118-13909-7
(EBK)
1. CREATIVE ABILITY IN BUSINESS. 2. SELF-ACTUALIZATION (PSYCHOLOGY) 3. CREATIVE ABILITY. 4. CHANGE
(PSYCHOLOGY) I. TITLE.

HD53.A384 2011
650.1—DC23

2011019566

PRINTED IN THE UNITED STATES OF AMERICA

10 9 8 7 6 5 4 3 2

RARELY DOES LIFE TURN OUT THE WAY YOU THINK IT WILL.

But that's okay — especially if you are equipped and ready to roll with it. This book is for those of you who desire to spend energy on making your life and your career all that they can be. Of course, we all receive help with that and I want to thank mine. Thanks to the team at Rule29, and especially to Sarah, Mackenzie, Jackson, Quinn, and Ava for being my inspiration.

Are you ready? Let's get to it.

ROADMAP

The path to balance always looks more complex than it really is...

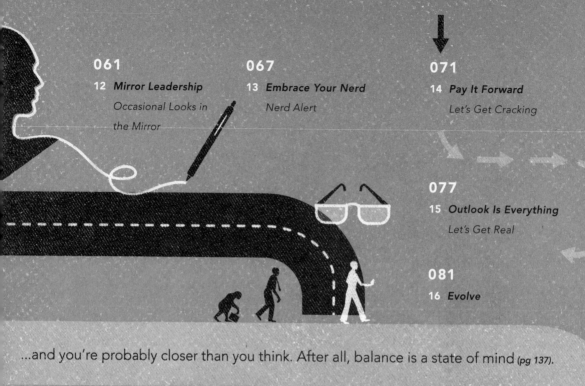

...and you're probably closer than you think. After all, balance is a state of mind *(pg 137)*.

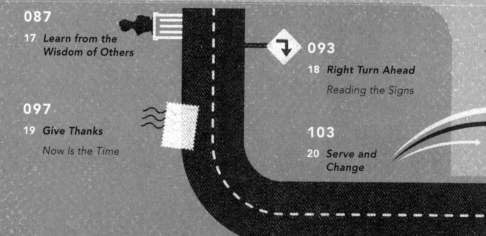

HELLO

INTRO

What is Life Kerning, you ask?
In graphic design, *kerning* is the fine tuning or adjustment of the space between letterforms (type). The changes may be small, but they make a big difference. A designer can go in and finely tune the space within a headline or a placement of a title so that a presentation is more enjoyable and downright beautiful to the reader. Or a design can alter the aesthetic part of a presentation, to ensure the material has the desired effect visually, beautiful or not.

In our business careers, we tend to think sweeping or wholesale changes need to be made to enable us to more deeply appreciate our lives

or our jobs. Yet it's often the fine adjustments between the smaller details of our lives that we neglect or do not revisit often enough that tend to make the headlines of our lives seem uncomfortable, not as harmonious as they could be, or just hard to read.

This perspective applies to individuals in all careers, without question. From time to time, all of us need to assess our personal and work lives to see whether they are feeding each other or fighting each other. This book is about you and these circumstances that will happen. It's about you the business owner, creative director, worker bee, cookie monster, creative problem solver, or just the person whose life is a little out of whack and needs a nice realignment. Regardless of how we got to this point in our lives, we're hopefully all doing what we were designed to do. When we were growing up, we doodled on our Trapper Keepers or on lined paper during math class and dreamed about creating or being a part of something that would be recognized and admired worldwide. Perhaps you haven't quite arrived there yet . . . or maybe you've made it, but "there" is not quite as fulfilling as you thought it would be. Perhaps you've even questioned whether pursuing that early dream was worth it. Was it really what you wanted? Did it even matter? My guess is that the answer to all those questions is yes, but that's what we'll explore in the pages ahead. I'm going to share some insights from my own experiences, along with some wonderful perspectives from others, and when we're finished, I hope you'll have gained some perspective on "balancing" the important things in your life or, at the very least, start looking at them differently.

Since nothing ever follows a direct path in life, this book is designed so you can, if you wish, peruse the table of contents and meander or explore the topics that are most important to you now. Or, if you're like me and, in some activities, order gives you peace of mind, then sequentially explore these thoughts and let your anxiety subside. Either way, as you progress through this book, you will see that you are wonderfully in control of the direction, choices, and next steps—not only in how you prefer to read this book, but in how you respond and in which steps you take next. Don't let routine, anxiety, expectations, or whatever excuse

you may struggle with stop you from
making adjustments; after all, you may
be closer than you think to your
life's goals.

...after all, you
may be closer
than you think to
your life's goals.

YOU'RE NOT

PERFECT

01

Okay, so it's not the most encouraging chapter title, but that's because we're getting right to the point: Some of your biggest problems are created by assuming you already have the answers. We've all been there, whether we realize it completely or not. You walk into a job or project and really feel like you've got this one. You say you are interested in others' opinions or feedback, but if you were honest, you're really not. Sometimes you are stubborn, you want to do this all by yourself, or you really believe you know all you can about the job ahead, or you may just not like your coworker offering suggestions.

At my first job out of college, even while I was working on my very first assignment there, I already thought I was the typography master and was ready to present my brilliant ad campaigns to wow our biggest clients. After months of hounding my creative director for an opportunity to showcase my brilliance, I finally got my chance. I was given the opportunity to put a direction into our pitch if—and only if— it made it through the internal critique. Man, I must have done hundreds of sketches (or at least it felt like it) until I finally came up with a couple of ideas that I knew were spot-on. I worked for days on the ad. And I reworked it. Then I started over and went back to my original ideas and reworked those.

Finally, the day of the internal critique came, and I was ready. I knew I had developed a couple of really great directions and concepts, and I proudly walked up to the presentation board with Napoleon-like confidence to pontificate my genius to my coworkers.

When I finished my presentation, there was an uncomfortable silence that lasted for what seemed like 10 minutes. Finally, someone spoke up and pointed out that the concept was solid, but the typography was brutal—and they killed the ad. Killed it. Dead. My heart sank. I had a brief vision of kicking the commenter where the sun doesn't shine, but quickly realized that might limit my chances for advancement . . . or for doing another ad, for that matter. Instead, I listened . . . sort of. I heard words and managed to mutter the occasional "uh-huh" or "yeah, makes sense" retort.

After the meeting I went back to my desk still feeling pretty devastated. Didn't my ad reflect the countless hours and endless application of brain matter? The brilliance was right there on the page! While I stared at the ad in disbelief, one of my art directors walked up and scribbled some font adjustments on the ad for me to consider.

I said thanks, thinking there was no way that was all that needed to happen. But I begrudgingly started refining the headline and organizing the relationship of the headline with the imagery, and suddenly something magical happened. I saw it. I saw what was missing, because those simple refinements brought the ad into a peaceful composition. At the next critique, my ad was selected for presentation and eventually even made it to publication.

Luckily, I learned early in my career that I wasn't as good as I thought I was. When you start thinking you have it all figured out, you let pride blind you to the obvious, and you may stop asking for input or counsel from others. The good news is, the problem goes away the minute you can admit you're not perfect and don't have all the answers.

Do you see yourself in this example? Do you ever ask for help? If you do, do you actually listen? Do you give credit to those who have helped you? The discipline of asking for, receiving, and then giving thanks for advice pays great dividends to those who embrace it.

No one is perfect. Embrace the mind-set that should be obvious: You don't know everything. We can learn from anyone, even a small child; we simply need to be willing to hear. Are you listening?

For your next project or meeting, make sure you get someone else's perspective, especially if that's something you don't typically do. How? By simply asking for it and setting aside your ego so you can receive it.

Responding to and agreeing or disagreeing with input is another key element in this scenario. Are you a person who encourages those who give input, or do you come off as guarded and resistant? If you don't know, ask a coworker or anyone you think will be honest with you.

02

When you're naked, it's hard to hide who you are. You require that kind of stark honesty with yourself about what you want from your career. This may seem straightforward enough, but take a moment and remember this morning. When you hopped out of the shower (I admit it, I hop), what was the first thing you did after you grabbed your towel?

Most likely, you checked out what was going on in the mirror. Now, you may like what you see—which means you are either (1) blessed with a great metabolism and have a great track record of clean living and self-denial or have accepted your shortcomings or (2) you don't like what you see all that much, meaning that you gave up on your workout regimen halfway through

January (again) and have some work to do.

Either way, what you see is the reality. No black T-shirts or vertical stripes to create a mirage. In the same way, use the content of this book with that type of naked transparency. You must be honest and fully admit and accept your areas of weakness and strength. Until then, you can't make great decisions. Don't let pride rear its ugly head; be willing to recognize and understand the factors that motivate you.

It is so easy to ignore that little voice inside of us that tells us the truth and then continually reminds us of what is really motivating us. But if we refuse to admit that we really *do* want that promotion, that new house, that expensive car (so we can look cool driving to work), more money, or trendy gear, then we really can't identify why we feel bitter, tired, or unsatisfied and consequently refine or tweak our behaviors to achieve those goals. Wanting those things is not bad; even wanting them for their coolness factor or as a status symbol isn't bad—*if* we admit how crazy or out of whack that can make our lives and how much work it will take to achieve them. Until we truly admit *why* we want certain things, we are never going to be able to effectively deal with the results or actions needed to attain those desires. It's vital that we monitor those inner desires and reasons and keep them in check.

I grew up with just enough materially, and my family frequently moved around. In one two-year stint, I attended four different grade schools. I missed a lot of the school year. When I looked around at each new scenario I found myself in, it seemed to me that most of my friends had more than I did. This made me very ambitious.

Still, I often struggled with shortcomings in school due to having moved so often in such a short period of time. I always felt like I had to work harder than most of my classmates. I never really excelled at anything academic—my talents lay in drawing and sports.

I'm not sure why I felt as though overachieving was important, but I did. Early in my career I was hungry, very hungry. I worked myself into a nice little workaholic lifestyle. Then, when I reached some of the peaks in my career that I had dreamed about, I found myself feeling empty, sad, and underwhelmed. Luckily for me, I took a time-out. *Why did I feel this way?*

The short answer was that I had never really been honest about why I wanted certain things. I hadn't owned up to what those desires really meant to my soul…to my life. I never got real about what I would need to sacrifice in order to pursue those goals.

You are never too young (or too old) to learn this lesson. Do you really look at yourself honestly? Ambition is not bad if it is filtered properly. You are wonderful no matter what you see, and you have the power to choose and change, but be honest (get naked) first. Then you can honestly understand why you may be struggling or feeling empty or making poor decisions— whatever may be holding you back from understanding your next career decision.

TAKING IT OFF

It's honesty time. No one knows what goes on in your head but you. Think about what you are excited about— desire, fear, love, whatever. Now ask yourself whether those things are worth it. What will it take for you to get from here to there?

Pretend you won the lottery. What would be the first 20 things you would do with your newfound wealth?

Now pretend you had just barely, and I mean *just barely,* what you needed to survive day by day for the rest of your life. What would you want to be doing?

There may be a lot to think about here, or maybe just a realignment of what you are hoping to accomplish in your life. Either way, it's time to take a look.

CREATE SPACE

03

The concept of creating space was the main inspiration for the title of this book. Creating space, aka *kerning*, is one of the main methods we use to add enjoyment to our day-to-day existence.

Most of us are moving so fast that we forget to take a step back (outside of the few vacation days we enjoy). Creating space is a habit. Like becoming a great typographer, it takes practice. Through repetition, recognizing what fits within a certain space and what doesn't, knowing which areas require adjustments and which are best left alone is all part of recognizing the right fit. To achieve any great kerning result, a designer must look at the letterforms close up, from different angles, upside down, and from a distance. Only then can the right adjustments truly be made. The same is true in life. Understanding where more attention is needed and how to make the correct refinements is an art form—one mastered only with time and practice.

In order to purposefully create space, you must give yourself time to step back and consciously think about *you*. Time to be honest with yourself about how your life is going. Time to look at what is going well, situations that are frustrating you, things you want to change, or ideas you are dreaming about. You can't allow life to become so busy that you can't work in some time to step back and assess how your life is going and what may need to be adjusted. And I don't mean taking vacations (yes, you need those, too)—I mean a purposeful time set aside to look at yourself and your life. Whether it's 15 minutes per week, a whole day every month, or a couple of times a year, create whatever space necessary to give you enough time to pause and be a student of you.

SPACE FOR TWO

I got married right out of college. In fact, my wife had two years of school left. I must have been amazingly charming or else my father-in-law had been drinking the day I asked for his daughter's hand, *because I really had no idea*. No idea what life was about to hand me, what with starting a new career, becoming a husband, sharing with and taking care of someone other than me, and having dinners that consisted of more than ramen noodles or pizza.

Early in my marriage, I was telling one of my good friends some of my concerns and fears about my wife and I evolving as individuals and as a couple. He shared with me something he and his wife did yearly that one of his mentors had shared with him. My friend had also married young, and he knew that living on love, even though it makes for a great movie, is not the fuel you can solely depend on. The answer for my friend and his wife was to go on "life retreats"—annual two- to three-day trips dedicated to talking about their marriage, their lives, and their dreams.

They choose a location far enough away from home that it feels like a getaway, but within driving distance so they can converse in the car and not get bogged down with the distractions of complex travel plans. The first day, they talk about the details and events of the past year—including the kids, finances, individual goals, friends, vacations, struggles, you name it. The next day they talk about the future. They make plans, create goals, and dream about what life could be like a year from now. The last day (or that afternoon), they do something fun, as a little treat.

My wife and I have been doing this for years now, and it is one of my favorite weekends of the year. Then, at the six-month mark, over a nice dinner, we create space to review some of the things we talked about on our trip. What's brilliant about this concept is that my wife and I start the year on the same page. We are approaching life together with an understanding of what we are each hoping for individually and what we want to do together.

SPACE FOR YOU

Because these experiences prove so valuable, I realized that I needed to create space individually as well, to devote time to focusing on my career and personal goals. I take one afternoon a month to assess where I am at with my work, my attitude, my personal goals, where I'm doing well, and where I need to put on my big-boy pants and go after my goals. During these times, I'm usually at a Starbucks, tucked away in the corner and listening to music. I take out my journal and just make a list of things I want to think through: *What have the last 30 days been like? What have I learned? Where have I failed? What have I done well?* It's often astonishing to look back at the previous month and reflect on what I was thinking, learning, or struggling with.

We are all works in progress. If we don't take time to look at the headlines of our lives and make refinements consistently, we tend to let life dictate our story more than it should. Create space and take time—you are worth it! Make this a regular part of your year, and it will produce positive results. All of our lives are different, and time, goals, finances, and so on add layers of complexity to creating space. Yet no matter your life stage or situation, we all need time to be still. Start wherever you can. The point to walk away with is really simple: *Just do it.*

 THOUGHTS ON SPACE CREATION

Just you: Creating space is only going to happen if you plan it. So schedule unbreakable time. If finding time is tough, you definitely need to work on that, but you can start by using times you may not currently use:

1 *Leave work early (or on time).*

2 *Utilize commuting time.*

3 *Try early mornings.*

4 *Take a half day off.*

5 *Use a Saturday or Sunday.*

These are just places to start: Spend at least a half day when you can. If you can work in time for a personal treat, do that, too. Go see that museum show you have been wanting to see, just *you*, at *your* pace, or whatever personal activities you are really inspired to do. Time for you is important, so don't feel bad about it.

YEARLY CHECK-INS

You have to get away. Turn off your phone. Go to a park. Stay at a hotel overnight. Put on headphones and huddle away in a coffee shop. Find a place that works for your life—one that ideally is inspiring and that allows you to not be distracted. When was the last time you were all alone and just dreamed? Dreamed about you? When was the last time you were just still, silent, and focused? When we are alone, we can really take time to be honest and tune in to what we have been doing well or neglecting at work and at home. Take the time, and take notes.

If you are in a relationship, before you do your couples' retreat, make sure you take time to prepare a list just about you. Then take some time and concentrate on your partner. You will find this to be an enlightening time no matter what you realize about your relationship. You can make it better by being intentional and observant.

BE ANTISOCIAL

04

It's funny that I'm writing about this right now, because while beginning this chapter, without realizing it, I've been on my two Twitter accounts, played a word game on my iPhone, responded to a Facebook message, made a connection on LinkedIn, and texted someone a picture of where I'm writing. No wonder I'm surprised that time has flown by.

I love social media. I pretty much have accounts on every platform just because I find it profoundly interesting. At my company, we consult with our clients about the best social opportunities out there, so some of my interest is work-related, but the rest is just gadgety social nerdiness.

But here is the problem: This ever-increasing, engaging, and addicting social lifestyle pulls us further and further away from much-needed focus on ourselves and our work and toward intermittent breaks for social interaction. It prevents us from having that sacred downtime that can help us feel normal again and not as though we're flying at a million miles per hour. Online and mobile engagement is both beneficial and enjoyable, but we all need to habitually unplug.

The more you engage, the more prone you become to constantly checking your accounts for communications you need to respond to. Soon time has gone by—in many cases, time that was just frittered. The things you intended to accomplish may be partially delayed, or you ran out of time because you were posting an update to your Facebook account and responding to comments rather than focusing on the task at hand.

It can be vital to use technology to help you manage things in your life where appropriate. But when you want to be more efficient at work or have more time, you need to look at the big picture.

One option is to regularly schedule parts of the day when you are unplugged. For you, that may mean forgoing phone, laptop, or tablet. For all of its advantages, overly accessible technology has affected us socially. The watercooler talk happens more often online now—unless of course you change that. Take time to handwrite notes, meet someone face-to-face, turn the phone off during a meeting, and concentrate on the moment. Being present makes us feel better connected than does our latest status post. Start with any of the preceding ideas, especially regularly unplugging parts of your day.

This accomplishes a couple of things. For example, it has helped me to pay better attention to conversations going on in my house. You will be more fully aware of what is going on if you are not having conversions in your head while you exist in a setting. Make sure you are fully engaged when you need to be. Learning to turn off technology is difficult, especially considering how accessible we all are now with the various mediums.

To see whether your focus and productivity increase, start a campaign for regular antisocial rallies. These can be attended just by you, or you can unionize your workmates—or your family at home. Either way, make a concerted effort to unplug and do something else. You might take a nap, exercise, work on your novel, or enjoy an uninterrupted meal for 30 minutes; any of these is a great start. Try hanging out with yourself, surrounded by pure quiet. When was the last time you did that?

What's interesting is that, when you do plug back in, you realize that maybe you are a little late to some of the conversations but that nothing happened is preventing you from still participating. The more time you take to return to the physical world around you and engage there, the richer your days actually become.

HERE'S HOW TO START YOUR ANTISOCIAL CAMPAIGN

1 *What times of the day are you most productive and tuned in? Choose those times to focus on the items you want to accomplish, whether it's at work or after hours. Unplug before you start.*

2 *Read something—not on a phone or tablet. Play a board game or a card game. Draw. Paint. Do something that does not entail an electronic device. Dust off the Etch A Sketch?*

3 *Work out and don't check Facebook, talk on the phone, or tweet. Seriously.*

4 *If your phone or tablet is just too tempting, give it to a coworker or family member for a period of time.*

5 *You can set aside regular, fixed times to have a no-device zone. This could be at morning meetings, at the dinner table, wherever. You might actually have some meaningful conversation!*

the POWER

OF THE

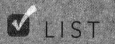
LIST

05

Most major issues in life can be solved, or at least put into perspective, in less than 10 minutes. No matter what the issue, when you sit down and take the time to write down the pros and cons or to create a to-do list, life becomes incredibly simple.

Many of us use the to-do list concept in our daily lives. I admit it . . . I have a list-making problem. The initial act of listing all the activities to be accomplished on a given day is sometimes daunting, but it's also helpful in remembering facts and tidbits. Then, as the day goes on and items are crossed off . . . well, that is list party time! In fact, if you do something that's not on your list, you should take great joy in writing it down and then ceremoniously crossing it out. At times, I hear some nice applause in my head on the wonderful progress I have made on my list as I cross things out.

When problems or difficult times arise and we are looking for answers, we often get so worked up or overwhelmed with the situation that we forget about the now. And the now is the power of the list. The past is the past. Let's learn from it—that's its magic. The future is unknown, period. Your list enables you to put those two elements in their proper place and helps you to visualize the now and stay focused on the very point that you need to make a decision on. A list also reveals to you the information you already have and what you still need to move forward on . . . whether those are items of action or inaction.

If you often find yourself involved in scenarios that are unpleasant because you tend to not think things through or you make decisions based on emotion, go get a pencil and a pad of paper and start writing. Make a list the next time you feel the urge to quit, to run into that meeting unprepared, or to call that frustrating client back.

Most lists can be made in minutes and are incredibly therapeutic. In this world of immediacy, a list slows you down in a wonderful way. Take the time to list all sides of a scenario—the physical act of writing is a very valuable exercise. Writing will help you to recall and remember the facts more clearly.

If you don't already have one, pick up a notebook that you will use exclusively for list making. This allows you to look back at your lists and reflect on how you made certain decisions and on which items you felt were list-worthy. Learning from the past is a concept that too often is underutilized. Reflecting on past lists and lessons now will absolutely produce a more satisfying future. Of course, you can also use your phone or tablet to make your list and track activities—decisions you are pondering, goals, dreams, your million-dollar ideas, or anything, really. Recording your thoughts is an invaluable exercise.

 LIST MAGIC

You can use the list concept on most of the thoughts and suggestions in *Life Kerning*. The only tip here is to go through each chapter and make a reflective note or a short list on each point and how it applies to you. Come back in a few weeks or months and look at them again—it will be an amazingly insightful exercise. You'll be surprised at how you thought about certain things just a few weeks earlier.

PLAY NICELY WITH OTHERS

06

One of my favorite parts of life is that there are billions of us, all having different experiences every moment of every day. While we are all very different, we share many similarities. One of the most powerful is that, by nature, we prefer to be a part of a community. No matter who you are, you desire community and collaboration at some level. However, when the focus is on your *professional* community, depending on the profession, the concept of collaboration often can only go so far.

Collaboration is very much a part of the process in most industries. As any creative will tell you, collaboration is a particularly large part of the process in the design industry. We work with copywriters, illustrators, photographers, other internal creatives, our clients, and other experts depending on what the job requires. But no matter what your profession, there's bound to be someone you admire whom you would like to work with, get to know better, or learn from. This is a natural, innate attraction. As humans, we seek out relationships. What better way to feed that desire than by connecting with and learning from someone we admire or respect, someone who most likely has different experiences than us? Learning from others' successes, failures, and strategies is a valuable tool that can help us design our own strategy and model for achieving our own goals.

With the proliferation of social media, you can connect with anyone on some level, but the collaboration I'm referring to is something more intimate and more specific. It's about finding others with whom you can get your hands dirty and do real work. One relatively easy way to start your first collaborative project is to get a group together and work for a cause or a nonprofit that you all are passionate about. You could also partner with another individual or firm when you think the professional outcome would be better with a joint effort.

That may sound scary to some. Because you are a business with competition, you need to pay attention to the bottom line, but money isn't everything. At times, it's wise to invest some of your work capital into new ways of doing things and learning from others, competitively or not. This investment could be in the form of money, time, or experience. Over time, you can enjoy your work more by doing it better— challenging your status quo, innovating, learning new perspectives, and being invigorated with new processes or creative thought. If this isn't happening for you, this is more important for you to try than you may think.

GIVING IT A SHOT

There was a definite learning curve when I first joined forces with other professionals. I had never worked with many competitive designers or companies in my field. There were well-known copywriters, illustrators, and photographers that I just couldn't afford to work with, so I did the only thing I could think of: I called them. My goal was simple. I wanted to learn from others I respected. I asked them to meet me for coffee. I wanted to get together with them and just talk shop. Others I stalked at conferences or professional events. I introduced myself and asked for their business cards. Over time, I worked on building relationships with these professionals.

Along the way, one of my clients decided to start a nonprofit organization to offer teens an alternative to the growing inner-city problems of crime and violence. Fortunately for this project, my client was well known, so this was a perfect opportunity to reach out to my peers at other companies and collaborate with some people I had always wanted to work with. This was a start-up with no initial funds, so my request was straightforward: "Would you collaborate with me, doing what you do best, for a great cause?" Amazingly, everyone said yes.

Throughout the entire project, I was a sponge. I asked questions; I contributed ideas; I was open to others' insights and perspectives. In the end, working with everyone resulted in the project turning out better than I could ever have imagined had I done it myself. Along the way I made some new connections and worked with some people whom I had admired from afar. The best part, of course, was that the result helped my client be successful. I learned valuable lessons in the process. While it wasn't completely smooth, I knew I enjoyed working this way, and I decided to design a way to do more projects like this.

Since that first project more than 15 years ago, I have collaborated on hundreds of projects. Additionally, with my employees and clients, I strive to create a similar collaborative, friendly environment. I have worked with others in my field on paid assignments, and we've worked gratis for causes that we feel passionate about. Cause collaboration is a key way to partner with others you admire, especially if your work culture is resistant to this type of thing.

 GO FOR IT

One of my favorite collaborative partners is designer and creative catalyst Terry Marks of TMarks Design in Seattle, Washington. He has become not only an inspiration, but a dear friend. He has taught me to trust and let others truly inspire the work being collaborated on. Following are some of the common pieces of advice we have given when we have the chance to speak together and evangelize about the collaborative way of doing things.

1 *Have clear goals and expectations. Make sure everyone is on the same page right from the beginning.*

2 *Take it seriously. If the collaboration is not treated like real work, whether you are being paid or not, the result will be less than what it could be.*

3 *Trust. You are working with these new friends because they are great at what they do. Let them do their thing.*

4 *Commit to this effort. It's not always easy at first, but be committed to the process.*

5 *Let the results inspire you to keep raising the bar for future collaborative work.*

6 *Learn from the experience and repeat.*

Good luck! You will be refreshed by the result.

No matter who you are,
you desire community and
collaboration at some level.

ARE *YOU* JUST

BAD AT

MAKING

GOOD

DECISIONS?

07

Decisions, decisions! The multitude of decisions facing you in your work and career can be overwhelming. Sometimes, depending on the situation, the pressures around the decision or your anxiety to make the wrong one can blur your vision. In order to succeed (at life and in business), it's vital to develop good decision-making skills.

Certain decisions require that you abide by a set of rules. In other words, you need to develop some fundamentally sound criteria that you can stick to, because the real issue might be simply poor decision-making skills. How many times have you made a decision at work and soon afterward couldn't believe that you made "the same mistake" again? Or at times, perhaps, your desire not to make the wrong decision led you to make *no* decision or to make a halfhearted attempt. This could pertain to hiring, firing, a job choice, or a project decision. Now, desperate financial times and an unstable business climate require some swift choices, but if you don't set up some parameters, you will make the same mistakes over and over again, no matter the situation. You will rationalize that it will be easier this time, that it's a different set of circumstances or a new client, that you've learned what to do differently—the list goes on.

I realized the need for rules in decision making when I accepted several consecutive projects, from a variety of clients, which everyone on my team (including myself) hated working on. As a business owner, I focused on the potential revenue and thought it would be better to take on clients and jobs, even if questionable, rather than turn them down.

As a young and eager new business owner, I attended a conference where one of my future friends was speaking. Sean Adams of AdamsMorioka was pontificating on the things he and his partner, Noreen Morioka, had done right. The spirit of this chapter is informed by what they talked about at that event and how I adapted it to fit my goals and business culture. I'm here to tell you that my 10-year track record of following these ideas has proved successful.

Of course, these parameters, or rules, will be slightly different and unique to each individual. It comes down to the type of business atmosphere you want to have and what matters to you. The following list of questions will help ensure that your work direction, culture, and decision making are aligned:

Will the work be profitable?

Will the work be fun?

Will the work help you attract other work, future employees, or attention in the marketplace?

If the type of work or client fits two out of the three criteria, you may choose to go for it. During a recession, it can be difficult to abide by these criteria, but it can also keep you out of potentially serious trouble when it comes to deciding what is best for your business.

These criteria may seem overly simplistic to some, but if you break it down, each question goes a long way in ensuring you adhere to your objectives.

Will the work be profitable? Whether you are a for-profit or a nonprofit, there is a currency and profit level that you desire. The question is simple: Will it be profitable or not? Yes, we've all done jobs just for the money, and these endeavors rarely work out. The big haul we perhaps envisioned never seems to materialize. Just being focused on the potential profit often leads you to ignore the signals of a difficult work relationship or unreasonable timelines, and it can disguise the amount of extra work that, in the long run, may not be worth your time, especially if it takes you away from what you are truly great at.

Will the work be fun? Having fun in your career is not only possible, it's a key ingredient to enjoying your day-to-day work life and being successful. Will this task hit your fun button? It's an important question. If the type of work, client, or project is something that you will do begrudgingly, or if you would rather have someone punch you in the face than do this work, then why do it? Somewhere along the way, many of us have forgotten that work can and should be enjoyable. After all , we spend the majority of our lives doing it.

Will the work help you attract other work or attention in the marketplace? Doing work that will help tell your company's story and promote your culture is the type of work you want to do more of. Winning awards and creating great PR are worthy goals, but taking on projects solely for this reason, without at least one of the other two criteria, usually tends to be shortsighted.

You can apply these same concepts to decisions you have to make in your personal life or other types of work decisions as well—applying different rules, of course! Consistently having three criteria seems to be the best litmus test for making sound decisions. Whether your goal is to help you live more healthfully, choosing the right person to date, limiting your shoe fetish, or making a family decision, you can apply the three-rule list to any area you are struggling with.

Your personal decisions should be based on the use of your time outside of work. Learn to say no when you need to, even if it's something you love to do. I love what I do, and I enjoy working

with people, but because I have an inability to say no at times, I had to make some rules to help me decide whether a yes response was even to be considered. Use the following list to determine whether an opportunity is worth pursuing. You need three out of three to say yes for sure; you need two out of three to consider the request; if it's only one out of three, you should say no.

Will this challenge you?

Will it help your business/career?

Will you miss anything important with your family?

We all want to make good decisions, and sometimes we just need a little help. You can use this technique to help you make better decisions. While there will be times when you just can't seem to get it right, creating a set of

rules can provide the empowerment
you have been looking for.

CREATING MORE GOOD

It's so easy to say yes. Just saying yes
feels good. But saying no can be just
as good, especially when it helps you
live the life you want. Saying no is
easier to apply when you have criteria
to fall back on, because you will less
often talk yourself into a poor decision.
As with anything, commit yourself to
working on it, because rules are no
good without some application.

Run your criteria by someone you trust,
someone who will be honest with you.
Sometimes our criteria are either too
easy or too restrictive, so be realistic
and upbeat about your list. After all,
you want to make decisions that push
you more and more to a positive place,
not to a place that will drive you nutty.

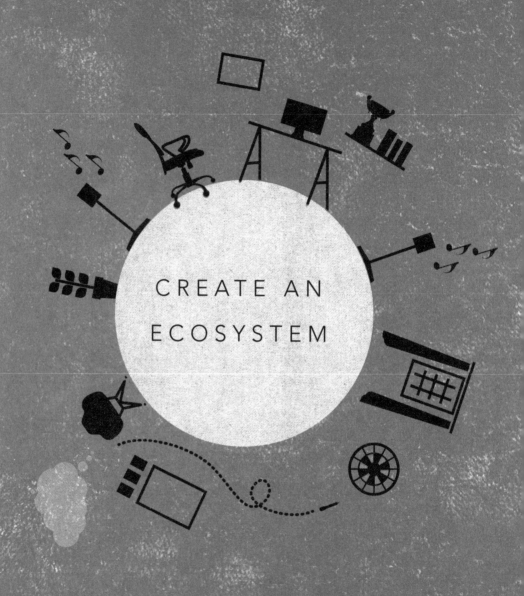

CREATE AN ECOSYSTEM

08

When I walk into some of my clients' offices, I get depressed for them—the ocean of beige, the horrific art, and the only environmental noise coming from the HVAC. I know that we don't all have the ability to make sweeping corporate environmental changes, but each of us does have the power to bring character, encouragement, and process into our workplace in some way. Some individuals don't bring a piece of themselves into their work environment. We spend the majority of our adult lives there—why not make our offices and companies as enjoyable as possible?

HERE ARE SOME COMPONENTS ESSENTIAL TO A GREAT ECOSYSTEM:

1 *A company that knows who it is and what its purpose is*

2 *An environment that is designed to emulate that mission*

3 *Transparency from top to bottom of the organization*

4 *Challenging and rewarding work*

5 *Employee involvement in key areas of company decisions*

6 *Consistent employee reviews and corporate reporting*

If you work for a company where the first two points apply, then you have the best building blocks for an enjoyable work experience. Working within a company that knows who it is and where it is going is essential for great team culture. If the whole team, from CEO to intern, can express why they are there and what the company they work for is trying to do, then that is a huge success. And if the work environment is set up to serve that overall company direction, then it's time to party—the good stuff is there.

In addition to a well-defined company, your day-to-day work area is important to your well-being. How can you make that more enjoyable?

Can you paint your office a unique, energetic, or soothing color? Are you able to listen to music throughout the day that keeps you motivated and focused on the tasks at hand? Can you create appealing community work areas—maybe a conference room or an outside patio? Is there an occasional break in the norm to inspire community, conversation, innovation, and fun? Much of the physical ecosystem depends on the culture of the company and the employees. It could be as simple as buying a new desk chair, gathering pictures or items around you that are inspiring, or taking a break and watching a quick inspirational, humorous, or educational video as a team. Whatever you can do to make your daily environment inspirational, motivational, and comfortable for you, do it!

The most inspirational item in my office is a picture of a friend of mine that was taken after we both got out of college. He was one of those friends that was full of life, always made me laugh, and challenged me to always be the best

I could be. Sadly, he died at a young age from cancer. That event greatly impacted my outlook on life. When I was reorganizing my office recently, I found that photo and had it framed. It helps me remember some important things: Work is not what I'm all about; I need to step back and look around daily; I should be thankful that I enjoy the kind of work I do; and, more than anything, I enjoy the life I have.

For me, that photo is something I respond to. Maybe for you it's vacation photos, Silly Putty, a Magic 8-Ball, a yo-yo, the soothing wonder of a lava lamp, Pandora playing in the background, or a gumball machine. Find things that you like to surround yourself with and bring them into your workspace. The combination of a company you are excited to work for and a workspace in which you are surrounded by elements that hold meaning for you are key ingredients for a great ecosystem.

 BEING ECO-FRIENDLY

Unless you are self-employed, you do need to take into account your teammates when creating an office space that is truly inspiring. Before you make changes or start a big overhaul of your office space, check out what you can do, and work within those parameters first. You never know, you could be a trendsetter.

If you are the boss, have you asked your team lately how they feel about their environment? Happy employees make a happy workplace. Have a conversation about what you can do to improve the environment. If there is a lot, create a budget and show commitment to improving things— you will be glad you did.

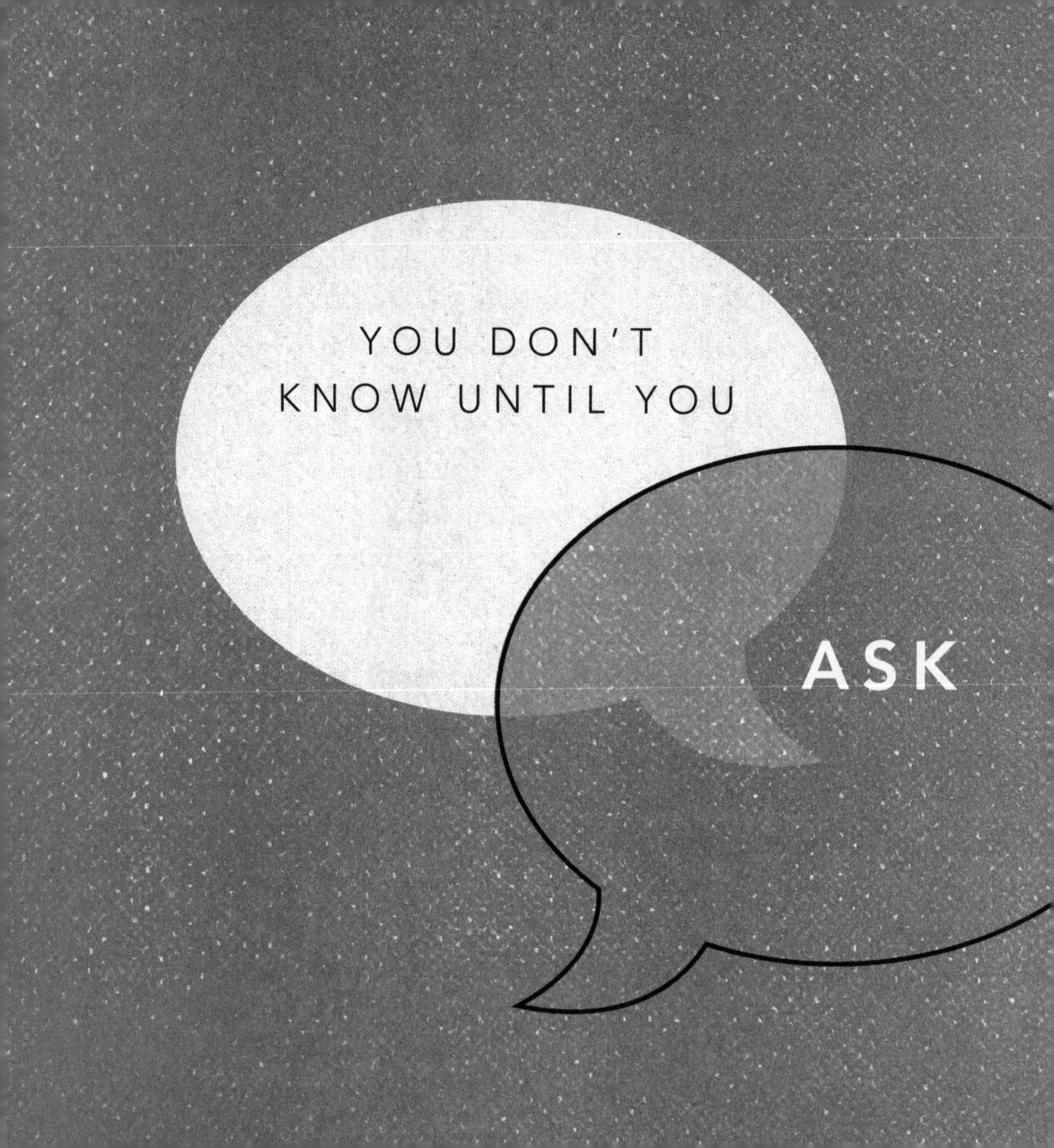
YOU DON'T KNOW UNTIL YOU
ASK

Once in a while, you will get some advice that you would be foolish to ignore. I've ignored this one particular piece of advice way too much: "You don't know until you ask." I don't ignore it anymore.

If you remember, when I first got out of school I interviewed everywhere I could think of for a job. I was lucky enough to have interviewed with my top choices right off the bat, but my first job ended up being with a company that wasn't even on my list. I tried to make the best of it, but I constantly dreamed of a better job with a better-known company. After a year of constantly trying to get a new gig and working hard for my current employer, I finally got my break. A position opened up at one of my top choices and I landed an interview!

Going into my interview, I was nervous but prepared. I had researched this firm's work and had asked around about the owner and the company's history. I tried to find out everything I could (which was much more difficult then, without the power of Google). The first part of the interview went great. I think my interviewer was impressed that I had done my research and talked about the company's particular projects. My excitement was building. At the end of the interview, the company was prepared to make an offer right then. A piece of paper emerged from a folder; a few things were scribbled on it; it was folded; and it was sent across the table. Looking at that folded piece of paper, I imagined a better opportunity, a real jump start to my career, and a salary that would enable me to give up moonlighting as a bartender.

As I unfolded the offer, my eyes were magnetically drawn to the salary. To my utter horror, the offer was less than I was making at the time—in a studio one-fifth the size of the one I then occupied. I suddenly envisioned myself jumping up on the table and karate-kicking Mr. Interviewer in the head, but I found my inner Mr. Miyagi and took a pause.

Luckily, I had been prepared to negotiate something much higher and had an idea on what my salary should be, so I smiled, folded the offer back up, and calmly said, "I would love to work here. I feel like I can help the company in a variety of ways," which I then listed. I went on to say that, based on what I knew of the market and this firm's competitors (which I named), I assumed my salary was going to be in a certain range. I asked, "Is there something I should know about the level of the position or your perception of my skills that would lead to such a low offer? Because I would really like to make $X." Mr. Interviewer thought for a second, reached over, adjusted the salary, shook my hand, and said, "See you a week from now."

Rereading these written words, the scenario sounds really cool, but to be honest, I was petrified and a little angry. I wanted that job badly, but I just couldn't have lived with myself if I hadn't at least tried to get a better deal. Now, most of us have the stones to negotiate a salary. We have some baseline expenses, and there is often some sort of benchmark we can depend on. But what about other areas of your career or life? Do you walk out of situations and then kick yourself for not speaking up?

I made a promise to myself after that interview that I will always ask for what I want, because you just never know. I don't want to walk away from a situation and say, "What if? If I would have asked, what would have happened?" If I had not spoken up, I would have had to mix gin and tonics at night to make ends meet.

There have been times when asking has not worked out, but that was more due to my poor ability to size up the situation. Asking has led to some of my best client projects and relationships, Super Bowl tickets, work promotions,

and starting my own company, to name a few. That last one may seem odd, but sometimes the person you need to ask is you. *What's next? What am I up for? What do I want to do?*

Don't walk away from a situation without asking. Ninety-five percent of the time, you'll be in the same situation afterward if the answer is no. What do you have to lose? Life is really too short to have regrets, especially if we are talking about asking a simple question. As with anything, the more you do it, the easier it is. You will start to establish the critical thinking skills to determine what questions you should ask, and you'll develop great radar about situations where you shouldn't ask—but again, when in doubt, *ask*.

Not asking the question and regretting it is a common experience. We've all had moments where we wished we had asked a question earlier. So, be ready, be brave, and speak up.

You just never know.

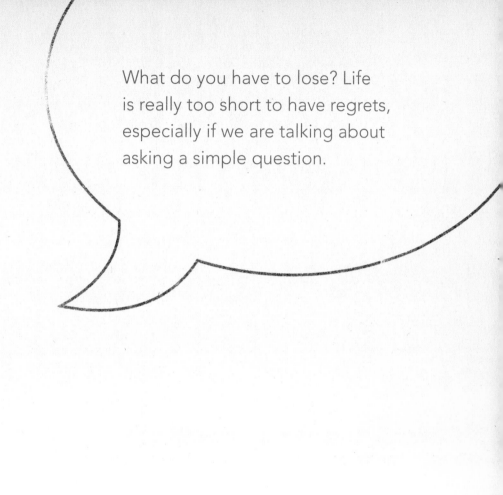

What do you have to lose? Life is really too short to have regrets, especially if we are talking about asking a simple question.

BE A LINK IN THE LOVE CHAIN

10

I enjoy meeting people and learning about their stories. That said, I never used to enjoy networking events; they always made me feel a little dirty. I can't say I'm a huge fan now, but I no longer leave them and go home and shower. I no longer consider meeting people at any type of an event as networking. It's more beneficial to look at it as genuinely meeting new people and building some level of a relationship. Whether it ends there or develops into an ongoing connection, or even a friendship, it all starts with being open and willing to meet others.

As your career advances, creating, maintaining, and growing your circle is immensely valuable—both to you and to others you can help. There may be times where simply being nice is an appropriate response to the social environment you are first trying to adapt to. Being respectful and professional will seldom make the wrong impression or get you in an awkward setting, as long as you're genuine. But if just being nice and shaking hands is what you call "making new relationships," you will be disappointed with the results. You need to have a clearly defined goal as you meet others, and pay attention to those you are meeting. Also, if you spend too much energy focusing on other people's motivations, it will detract energy from your own objectives. Wasting energy on things outside of our control is a common struggle for many of us. But if you decide to be a glass-is-half-full type of person and consciously work at helping others, you will slowly start kerning your perspective on others as a whole.

Simply networking with people who could put you in touch with the right people or organization can be really shortsighted. Kerning your perspective of this social scenario is a minor adjustment that actually has huge implications. Try to create an environment (or work in one) where helping others is just part of what is done.

When you help others, it should be done with no expectations of anything in return. This is a tough thing to do. Sometimes we put a great deal of energy into a relationship or share valuable connections to help someone, and we don't even get a thank-you.

Nonetheless, investing in others will often reap rewards beyond what you expect. I'm not suggesting that you only look out for others, however. You do need to be open and honest about the things you are hoping for when you connect.

However, before you can do any of that, you need to first go out and truly connect. Investing your time to be a part of your professional or personal community and to create, support, and promote your local circle of connections should be a part of your company's and your own personal culture. At one level, making connections—which is *not* networking— can be done easily enough via Facebook, LinkedIn, Twitter, or your preferred social media outlet. Making connections online is a good place to start, but true connection means you reach out to a particular individual and make that person more than an acquaintance or a number on your list. A network means that you provide information freely and offer your time and expertise whenever needed. It may mean grabbing a cup of coffee, some lunch, or a beer to connect and share information. It's taking time to meet someone and actually get to know that person. It's searching people out or finding time at conferences or community events to connect. I refer to this type of investment as creating a link in the "love chain."

It's not such a stretch to think about the layers or links in a network with the online social connections that we make. But if you think about your network as connections or, more metaphorically, a *love chain*, several things can happen.

First, you realize that you are just one link. Keeping perspective helps you realize that all links have a job and are only as useful and strong as the links they are connected to.

Second, the links closest to you are the ones you know best, and spending time with them and keeping those connections strong is important to the rest of your chain.

Third, the number of links you have or keeping record of what you have done for others does not matter. If you keep track or have expectations, your love chain is not going to be as strong as it could be.

Finally, I call this the love chain because connection is all about being genuine, honest, and helpful. Everyone who networks hopes to create connections that will help everyone involved become more successful. Be generous with your time, and when a scenario comes up, be a good listener, ask questions, find out what motivates that person, and see if there is anyway you can help.

Some people find this exhausting; it takes practice and deliberate boldness to forge a strong love chain. However good things happen to those who share, so get out there and start lovin'!

Try to create an environment
...where helping others is just
part of what is done.

DO WHAT YOU LOVE

11

When lottery numbers are announced on TV, I sometimes sit and dream about how I would spend the money. To start, I would get the money in a lump sum, take care of my family, invest, give a bunch away, and travel. Of course, I also wonder what my day-to-day life would be like. What would my job be? I would have to do something other than work on my tan. Invariably I end up deciding to do something along the lines of what I'm already doing. If you feel similarly, you're lucky! You're lucky to have found a profession that, even without the normal hurdles we all face in life, you would still want to do. Don't get me wrong—I wouldn't mind giving unemployment a shot sometimes, or try pursuing an acting career, but these are about as likely as my winning the lottery.

There are so many ways to look at life and how to spend your time in it. One of the greatest lessons I have learned from observing my parents is to *love what you do*. My folks never really did work they *loved*. They are both employed, and they work hard to survive, pay the bills, and be able to afford to take some time off here and there. They would leave their jobs in a minute to do something else if they thought it would be a better situation, especially if it could be in line with something they truly enjoy.

I admire that sometimes. I admire people who don't let their work consume them, who can punch out when they want, and work is done. It doesn't linger or wake them up at night. These people have their own set of concerns, of course, but something about their setup is attractive to me at times.

My question to you is simple, too. *Do you love what you do?* Let me add some detail before you answer, because, of course, it is a bit more complex than that.

When you ponder that question, try to approach it from different perspectives.

Does your job excite and/or challenge you? If not, does your current profession inspire you, and could you find another job within that profession?

Is your satisfaction with your job tied to your attitude? (You know you can change your attitude, right?)

Does your job allow you to do the things that really matter to you (e.g., taking off early to spend time with family, enjoying your favorite hobby, writing your novel)?

Does the type of work you do help to make the world a better place? Do you resonate with your company's mission?

Can you visualize a satisfying future in your current profession?

While *Life Kerning* is primarily about making slight adjustments and examining the various areas of your life to bring things together, at times bigger changes could be required. Spend some time assessing what makes you tick and where you hope to go in order to get a clear picture of who you are. A job or career change may be the right move, but finding what you love to do is step one. This assessment might just involve taking the steps to remind yourself *why* you are doing what you are doing. Think back to your college days, or when you first decided to get into your line of work. What about it made it special to you? What has changed since you began? Was it the reality of these things you only learn when you get into the real world? Winston Churchill said, "Attitude is a little thing that makes a big difference." Perhaps your job, where you work, and even the setup of your office are all good, but you just need to make a decision to enjoy them again. Or to catch some passion and let the things that don't matter go back into that space. If it's bigger than that, it's never too late to make

some adjustments somewhere to bring the elements of your life into a more positive balance.

 FINDING THE LOVE

Here are some more questions that may help you find the love again:

1 *What would you do if you didn't **have** to work?*

2 *How different is it than what you are doing now?*

3 *Remember where you started in your career. Go back to your first day. What has changed? Have you grown?*

If you really love your job, how can you spread that love? What might be the next step in your career?

MIRROR LEADERSHIP

12

If your actions inspire others to dream more, learn more, do more and become more, you are a leader.
—*John Quincy Adams*

What is your definition of a leader? Do you think you qualify as one? The short answer should be *yes*. If you are in a position to influence the behavior or decision of someone else, then by definition you are a leader.

When people talk about leaders, we often hear words like *inspiration, direction, vision, authority*, and so on. While these are all aspects of leadership, it is important to analyze and define your daily leadership habits. Too often, when individuals are in an influential position or want to be more obvious leaders, they stress about doing things that will be noticed, or have a major impact, or create a grandiose moment rather than on motivating or inspiring those around them.

We were each created for something great. It might not be "save-the-world" great, but you can still have a significant impact and be an amazing leader to those around you. A person's character can be summed up in what he or she does when no one is looking. The same holds true for how you lead.

Leadership can take many forms. One of the keys to creating the foundation for great leadership is to make your goal "the greater good." To put it more plainly, strive to be a leader who serves rather than one who expects to be served. What can you do to make your world better? Lead selflessly. What can you do, with your gifts, to impact the people around you and those you serve? This can be as simple as showing up a bit early or staying a little later. Or it might mean creating boundaries for getting your work done on time consistently so you can leave early or do something extra. Leadership might include *not* walking by something that everyone else just steps over, or simply holding the door for a colleague, or taking extra time to focus on mentoring someone, or writing a quick thank-you note, or offering a simple high five.

More times than not, doing the right thing, being honest, and working hard does create a fulfilling career and life. Handling yourself in a way that is worthy of following is the way to create the type

of leadership that has the most long-lasting impact. Instead of worrying about that big leadership gesture, ask yourself:

1 *Am I doing my core job as well as I can?*

2 *Have I compromised anywhere?*

3 *Am I helping define reality, or making it cloudy?*

4 *Can I be better?*

5 *Where could I innovate?*

It may be as simple as being able to look at yourself in the mirror and say, "I did all I could." We have probably all had someone of influence in school (perhaps a teacher or a coach) that made some sort of impact on us. When I was in high school, I had a basketball coach who was a screamer. He was six feet four inches tall, skinny, and a hotheaded basketball lover. He would get red in the face, (his face and a Coke can would match) spit on occasion, and chew out his players if they messed up. He also had a particular look that, when he shot it to you down the court, let you know that halftime or practice the next day was going to be unpleasant.

For whatever reason, I responded to his type of coaching. I had the honor of being a cocaptain of that team, and I often spent my time helping my teammates get over the verbal barrage that Coach had unleashed on them earlier. Two things happened to me during my experience. He used to scream at us before our games, "If you can walk off that court, look me in the face, and say you did all you could, then win or lose, I'm proud of you." That would seriously focus me and get me ready for a game. When I was exhausted, I would dig for whatever I could when I heard that in my head.

I try to remember that lesson when I think about my day. Try asking yourself what you can do to make what you're doing even better. It's not always doing the expected—it's taking whatever actions are necessary to achieve the best overall outcome.

Being a team player can sometimes be an unrewarding trait in today's workplace. These days, it seems to be more about how individuals can do things independently and be rewarded for that. However, often the most powerful impact you can have as a leader is doing your job to the best of your ability and helping to accomplish the greater goal. This doesn't mean that you go with the flow and act like a doormat; but own your job, speak up when necessary, give praise, lift up others, take charge of things if that's called for, take a step back…and determine what response is called for in each specific situation.

If you can look at yourself in the mirror and say that you did all you could, then it was a good day. Sometimes you will fail, but on those occasions what matters most is what you do the next day. While this may seem like a lot of pressure, we all require some motivator to keep us focused. If you operate from this standard, the rest (recognition, promotions, bonuses, etc.) will take care of itself.

OCCASIONAL LOOKS IN THE MIRROR

We all need to make sure we take a look at what is going on often enough to make changes and be effective. If you are in a leadership position, don't be afraid to have your team review you. Get feedback on the following:

1 *Your communication style(s)*

2 *Your strengths*

3 *How you can better serve your team*

4 *What they would like to see changed*

This will create a conversation that will help you to be more effective, evolve, and be in touch with your team. You can often do this as part of their review and tie in how you can work more effectively together.

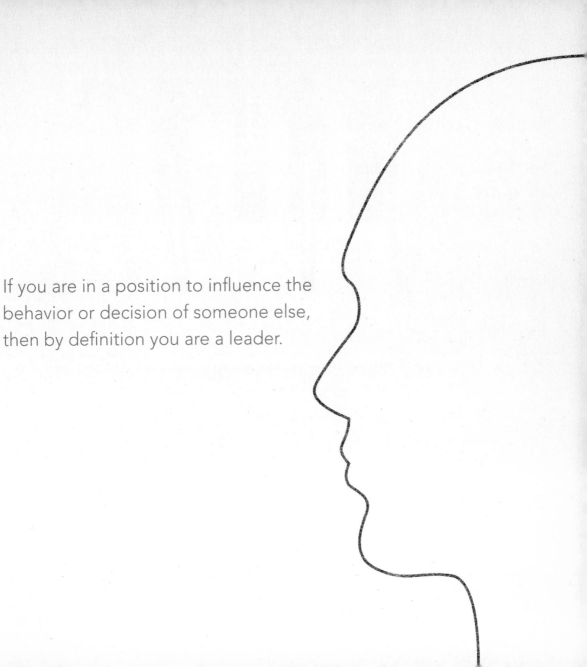

If you are in a position to influence the behavior or decision of someone else, then by definition you are a leader.

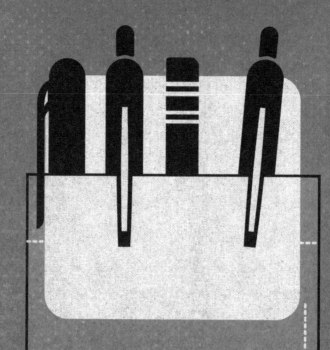

EMBRACE

YOUR NERD

13

One of the biggest revelations in life happens when we realize that all those things that we were in love with that made us unique early in life—things that we tended to keep secret—actually make us special and interesting as adults: the gifts and perspectives that only we can bring to the workplace. In fact, when you find a place to work where you can truly be yourself, something really magical happens.

The same goes for the group of friends you have. If you are in an environment where you can't be or aren't being yourself, then you won't feel truly comfortable or satisfied. Where appropriate, bringing the activities and interests that you enjoyed when you were younger (whether it was *Star Wars*, drawing, gangsta rap, or comic books) more fully into your life and work can accomplish a couple of things.

First, it can link you to a group of people you can have interesting conversations with, talk to about the Force, more deeply connect to, and network with; it can also help you apply new ideas to your job. Many of the most successful people were considered nerdy because they loved computers, comics, sci-fi shows, or gaming. Storytelling appeals to everyone because of its accessibility and its simplicity, and its depth in conveying messages. If you haven't read a comic in a while, give it a shot— or even better, unlock the mystery of comics by reading Scott McCloud's *Understanding Comics: The Invisible Art*. Taking the ability to convey a message in a short time is truly an art form, one that can serve you well in business and life.

If you are a nerd, it's okay. In fact, we all are nerds in some form or another. Have you ever thought for a minute that your nerdiness or dorkiness is a good thing? How many of those nerds from your high school or college days are succeeding in a big way now? Probably more of them than you might have guessed. Of course, it all depends on what made them that way. Some may be in jail or total social misfits, but the majority most likely are not.

Why do certain people succeed? Intelligence is one factor, of course, but the bigger factor is that they find professions that are in line with their passions, passions that have continued into their adult lives. While brilliance, a little luck, and good timing certainly help, your passion, which may have been mistaken for nerdiness at a young age, can help lead you to the success or satisfaction you are looking for.

Think about the activities you enjoy doing in your spare time. Think about those pastimes you just can't wait to do. Could these be part of your daily job? Are there any elements of these activities that you could weave into your job description? That could mean writing great blog posts for your company, bringing more culture into your work environment, or maybe even creating a new position for yourself at your company.

You have lived a completely unique life thus far. You are who you are because of your unique interests and experiences, and your individuality can make this world a better place in some way. When you stop being interested in things that excite you, things you get nerdy over, you lose a piece of what makes you unique. And that uniqueness can be a defining part of your life both at work and away from work. So, embrace your inner nerd. Start your bug collection, go to a Star Wars convention, begin your long-division tweetups—whatever it is, get going.

So, let's get nerdy . . . got any comics?

NERD ALERT

List three to five things that you think are most nerdy about you. Ask someone close to you to do the same thing. Are there parts of your nerdiness in your day-to-day life? If the answer is no, why not? If the answer is yes, can you add more of it to your day-to-day life?

If you are having a bummer day, get nerdy. Dust off those Star Wars action figures in the attic, buy a comic book, or resurrect your collection of old baseball cards. Stay in touch with who you are, because you are awesome.

14

I was interviewed for my first real postcollege job during the spring of my senior year. I had decided to take my spring break to do interviewing instead of doing keg stands somewhere in Florida. Because I had decided to move from the chilly Midwest to sunny Phoenix, Arizona, I strategized that I needed to get a jump on my competition.

I had done my homework. I had new shoes, and somehow I had landed interviews at all the firms I wanted except two. In all, I had 17 interviews— as I said, I'm ambitious. I thought, worst case, what great interview experience. At one interview after another, I showcased my work. I was passionate, dreamy about the future, and I made sure my future employers realized how excited I was to learn and do whatever I could. Most of the interviews ended with a handshake, a smile, and the usual, "Good luck, kid; don't call us, we'll call you."

After each of these experiences, I found myself dreaming of those aforementioned keg stands and sunburn. What was I doing wrong? I really wanted more feedback, some direction. Finally, on my final appointment, I pulled off my best interview yet. Building off what I had learned from the previous ones, I ended up out of breath and a little sweaty. I really wanted to show my passion and my desire to work.

After an awkward silence, the interviewer (who was a well-respected designer and the founder of the company) said to me, "This is the worst resume and portfolio I have ever seen. Wow, I would start over if I were you." I remember asking some questions, and then, while walking out, I picked up the pieces of my passion and broken expectations on the way back to the parking lot.

When I got into my car, I thought to myself, *What a jerk.* (Well, I didn't think jerk, but let's say I did.) I remember leaning my forehead against the burning hot steering wheel, which made me wince and sit back in the seat. I started laughing and crying at the same time. *Well, at least he was honest. Now I know what to do: I need to take four years of work and transform it into a pile of noncrap in two months.*

Driving home, I thought of how to pull this off. I bought a six-pack, and I made a promise to myself that if I were ever on the other side of the table I would regularly help others in my profession. If I were in the process of crushing someone's dreams, I would be honest *and* give constructive next steps.

We've all been there, haven't we? We've all experienced times when we didn't know what the next steps were in our profession, or we just needed some good advice. You don't know how much you know until you share it, and it's a refreshing and rewarding experience for you to do so. It's even more valuable for the person receiving the information. Sharing what you have screwed up, what you have done well, and what you would do differently is very beneficial, and there are multiple ways to share this knowledge. You could blog, regularly interview and mentor eager college graduates, or speak at colleges and conferences, to name a few. If you find yourself frustrated with work and life, add some Life Kerning; create space; and think about all that you have learned and experienced so far. Next, *try sharing it*. This will challenge you and make you better at public speaking and writing, or it will improve your interviewing skills. Either way you look at it, it's good for everyone.

Three months after that fateful last interview, I was back in Arizona. I had landed a job after fully revamping my portfolio and resume. That particular firm did not return my call or reinterview me, which was frustrating, because I wanted to show that I'd taken the interviewer's advice to heart, but I understood. Years later, I

collaborated on a project with that firm. A few years after that, I was asked to judge a show hosted by that firm. When I walked into the room and saw the past bearer of bad news (also, in some ways, my career savior), we had a great conversation. For me, it was a satisfying full circle; here we were, 15 years later, talking as peers. Had he not taken the time to tell me honestly what he thought, who knows what would have happened to my career?

You have that same power to help and mentor others, possibly changing the course of someone's career dreams. You have knowledge to pass on that will make the world and your profession that much better. It can be shocking to realize all that you have learned and can pay forward. It can also be rejuvenating, motivating, and inspiring. This type of paying it forward is often just the thing to help bring some satisfaction and energy back to your career while at the same time making an impact in someone else's life in ways you can't begin to measure.

 LET'S GET CRACKING

If your company doesn't use interns or hire a lot of entry-level workers, look to a local professional organization to see if you could (and would like to) become an influencer. Think about volunteering, mentoring, speaking, or blogging. Whatever your comfort level, start there. If no professional organization exists near you, check out at local chambers, professional networking groups, or online outlets.

Do you like to teach? Career days, trade schools, colleges, and universities are always looking for some real-world insight. Make some calls and

connections—you never know when you may be starting a whole new career, or at least a new passion! Either way, you can be a part of igniting someone's future career path, and that is just flat-out cool.

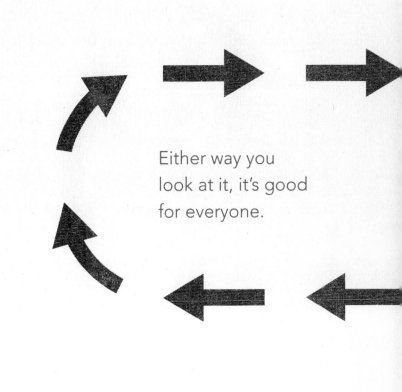

Either way you look at it, it's good for everyone.

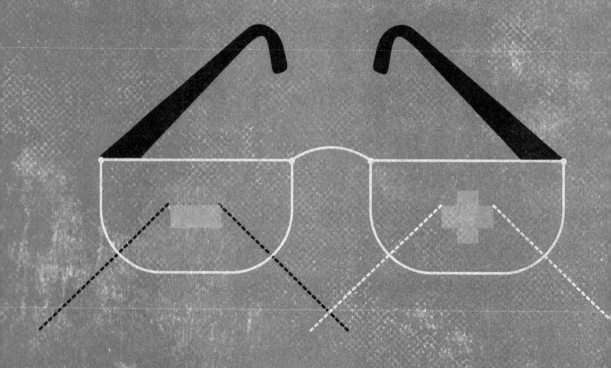

OUTLOOK IS   EVERYTHING

15

At some point in our lives, many of us experience terrible Sunday blues. We find ourselves not wanting to go to bed because Monday will soon be here, and that means facing another day at the grind. It can be totally depressing sometimes. One of the goals you should set for yourself should be to spend the majority of your career in an environment where you look forward to going to bed on Sunday night because you find your work inspiring, challenging, or just wait for it . . . fun.

Wishful thinking? Not necessarily. The implementation is relatively simple. First, make sure you are working in an environment that culturally fits you, and vice versa. Second, realize that your attitude, no matter what stage of your career you are in, plays a major role in your daily enjoyment. The fact is that life is just too short to go through the day wasting energy on things that are either out of your control, within your power to change, or just don't matter.

Typically, you tend to get upset because something didn't work out the way *you* wanted it to. Sadly, we all have the tendency to think the world orbits around our hopes and dreams.

When I traveled to Africa for the first time in 2007, I learned many valuable lessons. That first trip was to observe some of the work of one of our clients in the slums of Nairobi, Kenya, and Addis Ababa, Ethiopia. I would need another book to talk about all I experienced and the way it changed my life.

The one experience on that trip that blows me away time and again was meeting people who were so incredibly happy. Not happy with their situation, but happy that they were alive and that tomorrow is another day. For me, that was so hard to reconcile with the conditions that existed there. I remember interviewing a mother in one of the worst slums in Kenya; she was telling me how each day was so difficult—violence, disease, starvation, sickness, and poverty were constant. There was no relief from those factors being present every day. When I asked her how she did it, she said, "I take a moment at a time, and I'm thankful for the time I have."

Seems simple just writing it. Most of us will never experience the conditions that this amazingly courageous woman faces daily, yet our fortitude is challenged by factors much less severe than her unrelenting reality.

No matter what the situation is, *you* have the power to make your day as fine as it possibly can be with just a simple positive outlook. Don't worry about later this afternoon or tomorrow, concentrate on the attitude you have *now*. Tomorrow will be here soon enough, and there's no reason to worry about the past, other than what you have learned from it. What can *you* do now to make the present as fine as possible?

This takes practice, and it's easy to be drawn into your current way of handling your day—whether it's a pity party or a bitch fest. Make a commitment to empower yourself to be more positive in every situation possible. With a little practice, parts of your job will become more enjoyable because you take them for what they are—just parts of your day. With this refreshed outlook, you often find ways to change challenging scenarios or to realize that they were nothing more than just a much-needed perspective adjustment.

▬ ✚ LET'S GET REAL

If you are typically a positive person who lets things roll off your back like a *Choose Your Own Adventure* book, please proceed to the next chapter with a glass of your favorite beverage. Think about how you can influence those around you to have a change of perspective. Being a catalyst for a positive environment is not cheesy, it's a part of leading.

If a good attitude is an issue for you, have you stopped to really examine why (other than just flippantly saying you are frustrated with your job)? Is it really your job, or is it your stage of life? Have you talked to anyone about this at work or with someone who knows you well? Is work taking up too much of your energy?

Attitude, perspective, and joy are more often than not practiced traits or states of being. Just working on enjoying your day will kern things closer to what you are hoping for.

EVOLVE

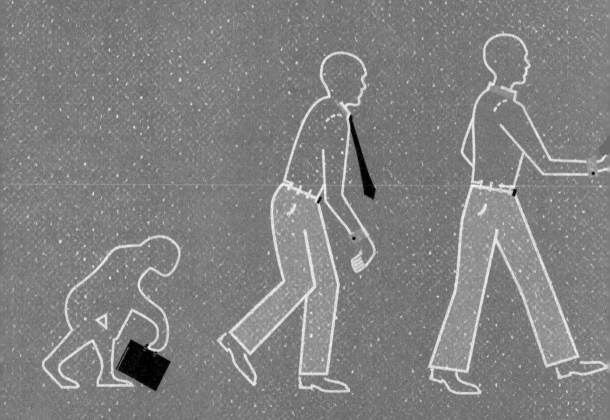

16

Many of us reach points in our careers where we become comfortable. That is not inherently a bad thing. Enjoying your work is as satisfying as dipping Oreos in ice-cold milk. However, it's dangerous to be overly comfortable in the sense that you don't pay attention to fresh opportunities, or contentment turns into staleness and lack of desire to try new things. Why? Because our world seems to be speeding up and changing at an ever-increasing rate.

Consider social networking, cell phones, and the way we consume information: Overnight, technology has changed the way we do so much, including reading, connecting, conducting business, overthrowing dictators, and so on. Being aware of what is going on in the world is crucial to being a viable employer or employee in today's world. Many people have created jobs or businesses around social networking. They have become an invaluable resource to their companies and clients. Others have stayed in touch with world events to the point where their bosses now consult them on international trade or perceived trends. Their personal interest in these topics has helped them develop a workplace advantage. Allowing these factors to change your work description, or even your career path, can be both scary and exciting.

Evolving can be subtle or dramatic, but it needs to be intentional. We are responsible for creating an atmosphere and the discipline for evolutionary opportunities to happen. This can take endless forms and can be somewhat dictated by the stage of life you are in. For many of us, new software and technologies that affect our jobs are coming out every few months. To stay relevant, consider going to free seminars, talking to peers, and attending conferences in your industry. If using these technologies is not part of your day-to-day life, consider supplementing your experience by listening to podcasts, doing personal projects, and reading blogs to make sure you understand the concepts at least minimally.

If technology is something that comes easy to you or isn't a concern, you may need to focus more on other aspects of your job, such as managing people or growing the business. Allow yourself time and opportunities to be inspired by people, to read books, to watch movies, and to listen to music—even though these activities take time. Plan your time and be creative to make sure it happens.

You can do several different things to accomplish this. Schedule time to read, even if it's during the workday. Lunch is a great time to close your door and read a book on your smartphone or e-reader, or go out for food and take your book along. Go to a few conferences a year to network, meet with others, or speak to groups. Encourage people at work share their music and what they are listening to for consistent exposure to music that you otherwise might miss. Organize mini film festivals at home or through Netflix, or take in double- or triple-headers at the theater.

The key is to understand what inspires you and encourages you to evolve, and then plan time to make sure you are being nourished in those areas. Remember, a healthy diet of inspiration and new things is crucial to your career development and your soul.

Start by thinking about which areas of your job you believe are the most valuable to stay on top of. Is it technical skills? World events? Personal inspiration? Social skills? Trends? The answer may be all of these at some level, but don't let that intimidate you. Just attending a few key industry conferences, reading blogs, or following some leaders on Twitter can really keep you informed.

Ask yourself what you need to do physically to continue to evolve.

Maybe it's developing a following on Twitter, speaking at a conference, or becoming a blogger. There has never been an easier time to develop a voice professionally.

The best mind-set is to always think of yourself as a lifelong student. This encourages you to have a craving for learning new things (without writing those daunting term papers). Someone very close to me had a career in warehousing. In the area where we lived, there were many major corporations that had warehouses. Because the area was considered a shipping hub, theoretically he was in a great profession. He began to notice that there was a rising trend to hire more and more migrant workers, and he started resenting some of the communication barriers he was having.

I encouraged him to take classes and learn a second language. My advice was, "Embrace the future; make yourself more valuable by being able to communicate with the majority of your workers so you can do your job, but also so you'll become more valuable in the marketplace." Sadly, he resisted. He was too comfortable in some ways and too fearful in others, and he let that paralyze him. Not capitalizing on that one opportunity left him out of work for years. The industry has passed him by, and he is now doing something else that he doesn't enjoy as much.

People experience many different scenarios, but the formula is often the same: Instead of being open to evolving or exploring a new change, individuals resist it and stay in a comfortable (or fear-based) cocoon— and then, bam, they become obsolete.

Don't let this happen to you! You are never too old or too experienced to learn new things, so kick the old habits to the curb and try new things as much as you can.

. . . our world seems
to be speeding up and
changing at an ever-
increasing rate.

17

Don't make decisions in isolation; have a group of wise counselors.

Read everything you can. Start reading about great leaders. Some good ones to consider are Abraham Lincoln, John F. Kennedy, John Adams, Harry Truman, Teddy Roosevelt, and Ronald Reagan, to name a few. What is particularly interesting about these individuals is how they went about making decisions throughout their lives and during their time in the White House. Name your favorite presidents and here's what you will find behind the curtain: a cabinet, key advisers, and a variety of people who assisted them. Everyone can benefit from a sounding board and the various perspectives that an adviser group can provide. Companies have boards, sports teams have assistant coaches, and presidents have cabinets. Why shouldn't you?

At times, no matter how hard you try, you will make some really bad decisions. Wouldn't it be great to rely on group of people who know you, who have had different experiences than you've had, a group of individuals you can discuss various scenarios with? The best part is that you can. You can create one for your company or for yourself personally. Here is a great quote from Abe Lincoln: "I don't think much of a man who is not wiser today than he was yesterday." We can all discover people who collectively make us smarter.

All of us have had to make big decisions, run an important project or a department, or be in charge of something that has many possible consequences. How nice would it be to have some people around you who would give you unbiased advice and feedback purely to help you in your decision making? I thought about this after I spent some time dreaming about owning my own company one day. I realized I needed some help. I had some great ideas, but I really wanted some affirmation and extra insights before doing some of the things that were simmering in my mind. I remember saying to myself, *"I'm a president. I should have a cabinet."* And that's when I started brainstorming about people whom I knew and deeply respected. After about 30 minutes, I looked at my list and started circling the people who knew me best, those who knew my company and would shoot straight with me.

I was also looking for a variety of perspectives and ages. After I made my list, I called my top three choices. I simply said, "I need some help, so I'm forming an advisory board that I'm hoping to share information with and that would then give me a timely and honest answer." I asked them to serve for two years and to be available quarterly and once a year in person… and all I could offer them was a thank-you and my reciprocity if they ever needed me.

Fortunately, they all said yes, and six years later, they are all still part of my organization. In fact, I have added a personal development element over the past few years. Now I share my business specifics with all of the advisers, and with two others I talk personally about my career and personal goals. Some great accountability, motivation, and sharing have occurred. I also serve as part of their advisory teams as well, and we have grown very tight the past six years.

An advisory board like this works only if you take it seriously and develop some parameters. Here are some things to think about:

Take it seriously. This only is as successful as you make it. Be open and accepting of both good and bad feedback.

Set guidelines. Make a clear list of what you are looking for and what you expect of your advisers. Having all of the parameters up front helps everyone make this a successful venture.

Ask for some tough love. Invite only those advisers whom you know will be honest with you. People who merely tell you what you want to hear will ensure that you stay stuck. Surround yourself with people who will challenge you—and choose those who are smarter than you.

Get ready to learn, network, reciprocate. You will get years of experience and knowledge; you will become a part of a larger trusted network; and you will have the chance to pay it back by being available to your advisers as well. Even if they are older and much wiser, everyone needs well-rounded perspectives.

Give quarterly updates. Your advisers are always available, but make sure you provide them with updates at least quarterly. This can be in the form of a call, an e-mail, a video chat, a meeting in person—whatever works. Location does not matter; consistency does.

Whether you are a president, a neophyte, or someone in midcareer, getting advice from others you respect is one of your greatest opportunities. Let me act as a temporary stand-in adviser right now: Get going! Make a list of candidates, ask them, and start. It will be one of the best things you have ever done.

RIGHT TURN
AHEAD

18

When people talk about leadership or development, there's a reason they talk about a *path*. We all understand that a path leads somewhere, and you can't start a journey without that proverbial first step, but we don't talk enough about the path we have been on. It is seldom a path we would have chosen or mapped out for ourselves.

How often do you look back in life and say, "Wow, look at how I got from there to here." Most likely, if you had read a preview of how that trip would unfold, you would much rather have taken a vacation or had another drink. We forget that our careers (and our lives, for that matter) never proceed in a straight line—it's always bumpy, taking dips, turns, and seemingly instant accelerations. It's important to remember that when we do find ourselves in one of those right turns, or our life is accelerating at a numbing rate, we have been there before, and we need to take a quick timeout.

We should get to a point where most things in life are not a surprise. Easier said than done. But as we plan our career or the direction of our business, we need to add an asterisk to our defined goal saying that we will adjust on the way. Having a perspective that your career life is an adventure and that you will take things as they come while trying to navigate the path you felt led to is important. It reduces your frustrations, your "holy sh*#" moments, and hopefully brings you closer to understanding which turns and adjustments are the right ones.

Every year, when you reflect on all the things that have happened and what you're doing now versus what you thought you would be doing, how do you normally feel? Do you chuckle? Do you cry? In the end, do you feel that you are doing something you love? When you plan your steps for the year ahead, go into it owning all your past experiences and making plans so that the next year will be better than the last, full of more joy and less gnashing of teeth, believing that somehow you can make this world a better place. Idealistic? Naive? The answer is up to you. You have choices along your path. Be prepared for the twists and turns ahead. Will you be prepared for the inevitable pitfalls, or will you let them

derail you? Welcome the challenges and, whenever possible, rejoice in what is going on. Those turns in the road define you. We learn best from mistakes and failures and how we handle those hurdles. Expecting them is not a pessimistic perspective; it's accepting the inevitable and preparing yourself to be ready. Welcoming failure isn't sadistic, but rather, indicative of a healthy perspective that you can learn from this and it will make you and your adventure better. So, strap on your seat belt and welcome the future! It will be different than what you think.

 READING THE SIGNS

Life is life. Are you prepared to deal with it? Understand that your day (or your career, for that matter) is a road that can be smooth, then bumpy; it's good to get into the habit of alternately turning slowly and then so fast you

have to slow down! This perspective
is vital for being prepared to handle
the future, in addition to being able to
enjoy the ride as you are on it.

The next step is becoming familiar
with those proverbial signs that mean
change is often around the corner.
Recognizing them and adjusting
accordingly will prepare you for
things ahead.

19

When I was in the fourth grade, I was a mess. I was sad, frustrated, and overwhelmed with all the change going on in my life. My mom had gotten remarried, and I was not a big fan of my stepdad. We had recently moved from the Midwest to Arizona, where I knew nobody. Before settling there, we had moved around a lot, and, as a result, I'd missed some basic building blocks (in math and English), and I was embarrassed about how much I struggled. All that really mattered to me was Michael Jackson's Thriller album, sports, the girl who sat behind me, and creating art in any form. I wanted to have friends, and I always made them fairly easily, but school was just hard for me this year, and I often felt humiliated and stupid.

My fourth-grade teacher, Mr. H., noticed me doodling all the time (thank goodness). He gave me a challenge that would change the course of my life. He told me to *draw* my next book report instead of writing it, adding that I would need to present it in front of my class. All I remember is sprinting home and reading my mythical creatures book (yeah, I was a dork—embrace it!). I started to take notes and tried to decide how best to illustrate this story.

Talking with a group of my friends a few years ago, one of them asked me who had inspired me at a young age. I remembered that fourth-grade book report. In retelling the story that day, I realized that it was a pivotal moment in my life. I was having a hard time at school, at home, and socially…I was really struggling back then. Then Mr. H. gave me an assignment that got me excited about school. This one observation on his part not only made me feel engaged in learning again, it changed the course of my life as an adult. After that initial book report, Mr. H. had me incorporate my visual approach to learning in different ways. Soon I was getting great grades; I was sharing more in class; I was picked as a student of the month; and, most important, I felt empowered and confident. I became a designer that day without even knowing it. I was introduced to my current profession and passion by a teacher who was paying attention. I'm wired to see things and remember information visually, and he helped draw that out of me. I didn't put two and two together fully until I discovered design

at college, but Mr. H. helped me see it was okay to learn and communicate differently.

My friends wisely encouraged me to try to find Mr. H. and tell him all of this. For some reason, I hesitated for almost a year. Finally, driving home one night, I thought of this story and started to realize more and more how important that experience actually was in terms of where I was now. I was ready to find him. When I finally got a number, I called and reached his son. He asked me some careful questions, took my information, and that was that.

The next day the phone rang, and as soon as I answered it, Mr. H.'s voice brought back a flood of memories and emotions. We chatted for almost an hour. When I told him how deeply he had impacted my life, there was a long pause. Then, in an emotional voice, he said how important that was for him to hear. He thanked me and we shared our contact information.

When I hung up, I felt so amazing that I wrote Mr. H. a letter and collected a variety of my work to share with him. The next day, I mailed the package and shared the conversation with the same group of friends who had encouraged me to reach out.

A few days later, I came home to find a brown mailing tube waiting for me from Mr. H. I was so excited—I thought it might something he was now doing in his retirement, or a gift of some sort. When I saw the contents, however, I was stunned. Mr. H.—for almost 30 years—had saved my art from that first book report! As I sat there staring at that fourth-grade art, I was overcome with emotion. Who could have imagined that, after the hundreds of students who passed through his classroom, he would have kept this? He also included a card that I had given him on the last day of fourth grade, where I had written, "Thank you for everything, especially for straightening me out." I had no recollection of that card.

Many of you may have had a teacher or mentor like Mr. H. who changed your perspective or your life. When was the last time you thought about that experience and how far you have come since then? Whether your story is dramatic or not, when was the last time you contacted that person and simply said thank you?

Saying thank you is *never* a bad thing.

NOW IS THE TIME

Who you are today is not purely your doing. A collection of people and experiences have shaped you. Take some time to express your thanks. Handwritten letters and phone calls are far better than e-mails. But do what you can; it's important and powerful.

If the person you want to thank is gone, thank that individual anyway and share this with his or her family, or tell the story to someone who cares about you. It's important for us to acknowledge those who help change our world.

Who you are today is not purely your doing. A collection of people and experiences have shaped you. Take some time to express your thanks.

SERVE AND CHANGE

20

Want to change the way you do things? Serve others.

Each of us is here to do something other than just work. Don't get me wrong, our work is important, even if it merely serves to meet our basic needs. But we are all a part of something bigger, and we are designed to play a unique part in that larger community. Maybe this is the area of your life that needs the most attention; it might even be time for a reboot.

This is a topic worthy of discussing, because most of us at some point encounter a nagging sense of doubt that causes us to question what this whole rat race is about anyway. Defining your purpose really helps

align and adjust work and put it in its proper place.

Even for the smallest changes in our lives, there often needs to be a change of perspective, a proverbial shock to the system, a "realigning of the soul." This may sound daunting, but while passion is such a consuming fire, such a fuel for action, it also can be an evil companion that beats you into exhaustion. One of the best ways to become energized, to have your passion renewed or redirected, is to help others. I'm referring to helping with no expectations. It's not about doing it for marketing purposes or to look good to your advisers, your employees, or your friends. Help others because you truly want to give of yourself. Otherwise, I'm of the opinion that you don't truly give—or gain—to the fullest.

Doing one thing at a time is a good place to start. One day, I walked into the office, looked at the work I was doing, and realized it was just temporary. I wasn't doing anything to really change the world in any way, shape, or form. I began trying to find organizations that I could do work for in my area of expertise as a means of helping. In doing so, I've met some amazing people and organizations, and I've helped them do impactful and world-changing work.

For some of you, serving by using your talents in your full-time job may be all you have room for in your life right now. And that's okay, too. Everyone has skills and gifts that can help others in

some way, shape, or form. Set a goal to find a way to start sharing yours. Give blood. Work at a food bank or a soup kitchen—and not just during the holidays when everyone else wants to. Volunteer at a hospital or a nursing home. Read to kids at a library. Go out and meet the needy in your own neighborhood. Whatever causes your heart to ache, wherever you see a need, or whatever bothers you about the world, get involved.

My team and I work with a partner organization to bring awareness about sub-Saharan Africa, one of the poorest areas of the world. Injustice, starvation, and sickness are the daily realities there. And even though I want to do more "dirt-under-my-fingernails" work there, we serve these areas better by using our work talents. Doing this has given me a new perspective in my daily life. It has reminded me that when I can serve, I need to serve—whether it's holding a door, packing food for those in need, helping my community in some way, or getting out of my comfort zone to serve those who are "different" than me.

Being in Africa has humbled me in ways that I needed. The fact that there are people in our world just hoping to live until the next day is inconceivable to me. Knowing that there are kids who are born, live, and fight for survival on the streets is unthinkable to me. Seeing what so many in the world deal with helps to balance the often insignificant things I stress out about.

For you, the reminder may not need to be so dramatic. But experiencing Africa has helped me look at the world through a different lens—a lens that helps me see the world as a much smaller place, a place where we can all do something.

Make sure you love what you do, and if you do, appreciate that you can make a living doing it. Discovering ways to do what you're made for will help make this world a better place, but in the end, keeping work and life in perspective is what's important. Serving in the larger community also gives you the lens to serve in your workplace—serving your boss, your peers, and your clients in a way that honors them. All the awesome goodness that comes from serving others is simply icing on the cake.

So, how can you serve? Or, if you already have found outlets for helping others, how can you serve in a new way, maybe something outside of your comfort zone? It will change the way

you see the world. It starts with saying
yes and getting out of your chair. Get
up and say yes to something today.
Work will still be there tomorrow.

Even for the smallest changes in our lives, there often needs to be a change of perspective, a proverbial shock to the system, a "realigning of the soul."

YOU CAN BE GREAT

ANYWHERE

21

Depending on your profession, often the city you work in or the company you work for is part of the package. We all identify ourselves with what we do to a certain extent, and taking pride in what we do is good. But when our level of enjoyment or the meaning of what we do is based on where we work and who we work with, that might be something we should take a look at.

In most professions, big cities are seemingly very important, especially New York. We believe if we want to be somebody, we need to move to Los Angeles, New York City, Chicago, or the latest hot city in the industry magazines.

The thinking is that if you work in a big city, with a big-name firm, somehow that makes you exponentially more likely to succeed. The reality is that you can be great anywhere—and, more important, true success is defined by what *you* think is valuable, not what the world around you dictates.

The allure of success and fame is tempting for anyone. But if we are honest, those pursuits can often lead to empty and regretful paths along the way. I'm not saying you shouldn't aim to be the best at what you do or to have an admirable reputation. Doing your thing to the best of your ability should always be goal number one. If and when those other side benefits or accolades happen, they will be more enjoyable because you didn't have to sell your soul to get there.

My company is in a nice, quiet suburb of Chicago. I tell people I work in Chicago when I'm traveling because they have never heard of my town. I'm used to the sudden downgrading or lowering of previous perceptions when some find out I'm not actually *in* the city. That used to get me pretty worked up, until I realized that my team and I are happy where we are, so why should I care what others think?

Of course, we still want people to respect what we do, and perhaps we would get more press or even more respect if we were located in the city, but honestly, I don't care, because I'm content. Some of those professional highlights you may think are so important really don't matter, either. What matters is that you're doing something you love, with people you like, for a company that you are aligned with culturally and that is striving to work with the right type of clients.

With today's technology, you can do your thing in the middle of a jungle if you have access to the Internet. Location is less and less of a factor these days. Who really cares who is on your company's client list? Is your work fulfilling? Do you enjoy it? Are you paid a fair wage? If you can answer yes to these three questions, is there really an issue?

The "grass-is-always-greener" complex sneaks in at times. Moving on may be the right decision at some point because you may have hit the ceiling where you are currently. However, more often than not, *staying* can be more challenging and require more skill development. Pushing yourself to learn or to create new skills for your position might be the most fulfilling thing you can do—and if you are lucky enough to collaborate with others, it can be the best of both worlds. The appeal of having big clients and what some of those relationships can enable you to do is a wonderful thing, but it does *not* guarantee work happiness. Often, the greatest satisfaction comes from helping smaller clients, because you can see the results of your efforts in a more palpable way.

Whether you are in midtown Manhattan or in a town with a population of 29 people is not of consequence if you love what you do. Have dreams and aspirations, but don't allow your idea of success or failure to be focused on location. If you are good, talent has a way of attracting more opportunity, because people like being aligned with those who are successful. So keep doing your thing—no matter where you are.

22

Why do we do what we do? You've probably woken up at some point in your life and said to yourself, "What's it all about anyway? Do I really need to go in today and deal with the same old stuff?"

Even if you have the greatest job in the universe, moments like this have a way of seeping into your mind occasionally. But if thoughts like these linger, or if you are looking for a new perspective, here is the perfect suggestion: Find something to believe in—something that is bigger than you.

In the end, work is just work. What is guiding you to make the choices you make? Your passion? What you think is right? Your friends? Your faith? Whatever your outlook, believing in something bigger than you helps to put all of the aspects of your life into perspective. We all have something that guides us, something that we are meant to pay attention to. Along the way, it's important for us to figure out what our priorities are and keep ourselves in check.

We are here to do something other than just work. Our work is important, even if it merely serves to meet our basic needs, but we are all a part of something bigger, and we are designed to play a unique part in that community. Maybe this is the area of your life that needs the most attention; it might even be time for a reboot.

This is a topic worthy of discussing

because most of us at some point encounter a nagging sense of doubt that causes us to question what this whole rat race is about. Getting some definition of that for yourself really helps align and adjust work and put it in its proper place.

What that actually means for you is part of the adventure. Start, restart, or continue to pay attention to what is bigger than you. It will provide the ultimate clarity that helps you sleep at night and gets you out of bed in the morning.

People on their deathbeds do not wish that they had worked more. When reflecting on their lives, they may wish they had loved, played, explored, served, and lived more instead of working so hard chasing fame and fortune. If you don't have a job that fuels your life or live a life that fuels your work, then look at your focus, your reason for doing, your passion . . . the answer lies there.

 HOW TO LOOK AT BELIEVING BIGGER

Do you have passion in your work? In your personal life? If the answer is yes, then can you do more of that? If the answer is no, how can you add some of that back into your life?

If work is causing your life to be blurry, upside down, empty, shallow, or meaningless, it's time to call a timeout. Why are you doing what you are doing? Remember the things that fueled your passion and go back to them. What adjustments can be made? Don't be overwhelmed—you can do only one thing at a time, but the path needs to start somewhere, so move where you feel led to go.

23

Some of the best moments in life are those when we can completely unplug and unwind. Traveling can provide inspirational moments for you, because when you are completely away from your normal life, you don't have the daily distractions and your mind opens up. When the fresh breeze of relaxation flows in and the stress and anxiety of our daily grind blow out, we are left with an openness that all too often tends to get locked away in a room somewhere.

Whatever style of vacation you enjoy, the key is to relax and allow yourself to be exposed to different things. Times like these provide experiences, sights, sounds, and culture that are different from the daily grind. This is true whether you are in Paris, Des Moines, or Saskatchewan.

Try to unplug as much as possible. It may take a day or two to truly let go of the pace and distraction of your day-to-day world. But you will soon start to feel refreshed and clearer on life as a whole. Now, you may be reading this and thinking, *"This can't be more obvious—of course we all need this."* But many people *never* take a break. Or if they do, it's a day or two at a time. That's an unhealthy pattern. Vacations provide breaks from routine, and they allow us to focus on smaller details and bigger goals that we may be neglecting or putting off in our day-to-day lives.

Traveling to new places gets you out of your comfort zone and reminds you that life is much bigger than your day-to-day routine. New scenery and cultures show you that life is full of variety, and that yours can be full of variety, too—if you allow it to be. Sometimes that small reminder is all you need to be more appreciative of what you have or to realize that it's time for some sort of adjustment.

Even if you can't get away for a week to a distant locale, you can start by taking one day each month to focus on your work and how you're feeling about it. It doesn't even have to be a vacation day—it can be a Saturday, a Sunday, or even a collection of nights after work. Then, when you are able to plan a vacation, try to bring a greater level of relaxation…a beach, an adventure, or any new place you've yet to explore. These types of plans sometimes provide the perspective, the energy, and the focus you need to get through a rough work stretch, and they also offer an opportunity to take a timeout, to take a breather. Life is about so much more than work! Pack your suitcase and get out of Dodge. Go to Europe, South America, the Caribbean, a state or states you haven't visited yet—start making some plans and get going!

Whatever style of vacation you enjoy, the key is to relax and allow yourself to be exposed to different things.

THE POWER OF

A NAME

HELLO

I had a profound experience on a trip to Nairobi, Kenya, that totally changed the way I think about communication. I was on a trip to film a documentary about the reality, injustice, complexity, and utter depth of extreme poverty in and around that part of Kenya. As art director and producer, I was working with the team to help coordinate the style, the story, and the on-the-ground logistics.

On the first day, we kept all the equipment at our home base and went as a team for a walk through the slum areas. Our team's coleader thought it would help us prepare for our first full day of shooting to see the terrain and to meet the people whose story we would help give a voice to. Our senses of sight and smell were attacked right away when we opened the van that first day and took in the scene before us. As far as we could see, there were corrugated, rusty shacks, mud, and people everywhere. As we stepped out of the van, we experienced the unforgettable, ever-present smell that clings to the slums—an unmistakable mixture of garbage, human waste, and life's activities, all swirled together to form an indelible stench, one that burns your eyes and stays with you long after you leave.

We weren't 10 paces into this scene before we had 20 to 30 kids running around, greeting us in a mixture of Swahili and broken English. They grabbed our hands, followed us around, and ran to get more of their friends. It was overwhelming, even more so because I was trying to keep focused as I looked around at the scenery and tried to imagine how we were going to get our shots and what else our crew might need that I hadn't thought about yet.

One team member, Bruce, kept stopping to play with the kids. He would distract them as we were trying to organize some thoughts on our shoot the next day. He then would gather them in a group and try to talk to them and learn their names. It was funny at times to hear the *mzungu* (Swahili for "foreigner") talk to these beautiful kids who couldn't fully understand what he was saying. After we had done our scouting and heard some sobering stories and viewed some even more sobering realities of

that area, we all played with the kids for a while and left.

That night when we got back to our base, we had a group meeting. We sat and talked about how tough this place was and what struggles the next day had waiting for us. As daunting as it was, though, we were all energized to tackle this project, and we went to bed in high spirits. The next day came and it was, as we expected, a tough, tough day. We continued to see, hear, and experience situations that were just unimaginable.

That night, as we sat around sharing tales about our day and discussing the next day's shoot schedule, Bruce told us a story that brought all of us to tears. It was the simplest of reminders about how important and valuable our daily communication is. Bruce shared that when he arrived on the scene that morning, some kids ran up to him from the night before, and he greeted them by name. He described the look on these beautiful kids' faces and the change in their body language – all because someone had remembered them and called them by name. In that brief moment, he had made a connection with the children and had brought a moment of happiness to their difficult lives.

I share this story because it's so easy to forget about the power of a name. We all like to be recognized and called by name. Remembering the names of those you work with or for is incredibly powerful and important. It's more than name recognition. Bruce took the time and effort to form a relationship with these kids; he paid attention and was truly engaged. He could have stayed with the group and let someone else do it, or he might have yelled at the kids to barricade them from us, but instead he sat with them. He played with them. He knelt down, made eye contact, and talked to them face-to-face.

All too frequently, we forget to do that. With e-mail, texting, and online chatting, we miss the opportunity to form more intimate relationships and truly learn people's names. This type of personal interaction is invaluable in both our personal lives and the workplace. Take the time to learn about the people around you, on whatever level that is appropriate. You're at work for the majority of your time—you want people to know and recognize you for who you are, and you should do the same for them.

I know that if Bruce could have, he would have tried to learn all the names of the hundreds of kids with whom we interacted for those two weeks. To him, it was just a natural extension of the kind of man he is. My favorite part of this story is that when we left each night and waved good-bye, there was only one name I heard from most of the kids: "Bye-bye, Bruce!"

What a great goal to have in all areas of life, and especially in the workplace: Treat others as you would like to be treated. And it all starts with a name.

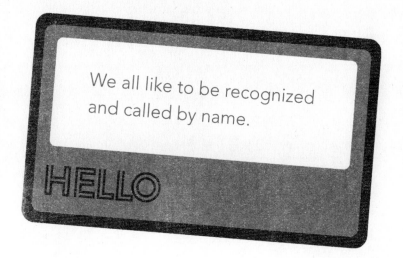

We all like to be recognized
and called by name.

HELLO

DO
PERSONAL
PROJECTS

25

What part of your job gets you most excited about the work that you do? What inspired you to get into your profession in the first place? How can you live a life that inspires your work and work in a way that inspires your life?

Whether you call it a work hobby, a personal avocation, or a top-secret initiative, doing a personal project for work is a good thing—a very good thing. It's definitely beneficial to serve outside of work using skills beyond your work skills, but doing a project that makes you better at your job is equally valuable. No matter what your job entails, there is definitely some personal project you can undertake that makes you better or reignites a spirit that may have been waning professionally.

In the creative field, coming up with those personal projects is a little more obvious than in other professions. Having personal projects outside of work can provide an outlet creatively that work doesn't allow or that we want to do more of. That could be making posters for our favorite local band, doing personal photography projects that challenge the way we see things, creating personal websites, or learning or retuning to playing an instrument. Whatever the activity, it should allow you to explore, learn, and become better at your creative craft. These personal projects are primarily for our own soul's nourishment, but projects like these can also lead to great career moments. Personal projects offer many options that you may not get all the time at work. With a personal project, you can do whatever you want however you want. Doing something different can influence or improve the way you, and perhaps your company, do work. Personal projects can help you develop new techniques. Additionally, these projects can show you whether you have a particular style of doing something. Whether your technique is good or bad, often a personal project can give you the best example of how you approach your work, enabling you to learn without the stress of someone breathing down your neck.

A personal project should be fun and challenging—challenging in the sense that you choose to do the project only because you want to, and you want

it to be different than what you do at work. But in challenging yourself, make sure the project is inherently enjoyable. This challenge-to-fun ratio is often the element that has dimmed at your day-to-day work, but it is ultimately one of the reasons you got into your profession. Being able to recall that feeling can improve your daily work experience—or at the very least help you identify ways to bring that feeling to your workplace.

Personal projects can bring new perspectives to the workplace, result in job promotions, and even create new companies, but more than anything, uncovering or returning to a passion alone is extraordinarily fulfilling.

I started a personal blog, hoping that it would make me be a better writer and allow me to work out some thoughts I had on business. Doing this led me to come up with some ideas for talks that I ended up presenting at conferences. Blogging helped me to explain in a much more powerful way how my company approaches our work. It also launched my desire to write a book. If I hadn't pursued this particular personal project, you wouldn't be reading this now, and I would still be dreaming about writing a book someday on a subject that I care about very much.

So, what personal project could *you* do? What passion lies in you that is begging to get out and party? Make it happen, and see what comes of it.

FOCUS ON STRENGTHS

26

Do you ever think, "Man, I'm really good at this or that"? Often, we focus too much on what we want to change about ourselves; we think that if we can just fix that one thing (lose weight, get a different job, or whatever that thing is), all would be a little better. There may be some merit to that, but what about focusing on what you are great at? We tend to focus on our weaknesses or on things we would like to change.

Change should be an ongoing process, but sometimes there is a precipitating event that makes us realize we need to change. There usually comes a point in your career when you will find yourself bored, frustrated, or desiring a change. A change may be the right thing, or you may need an adjustment, a reminder of why you do what you do and what is most important in your life.

The constant barrage of messaging that we are inundated with daily about ways that we can be happier, look better, and be richer doesn't help you see your strengths. We live in a world focused on constant change as a way to a better life. Image, desire, fear, and sex sell—they create scenarios of want. No matter what your profession, most of us are constantly trying to attract people to our product and services, but it's important that there is truth in how we sell our products and services, because *truth* builds relationships better than any manipulation.

One of the foundations of truth is *strength*. When we focus on our strengths, we establish a firm foundation to build on and evolve. The key is identifying what those strengths are and accepting them. Focusing on these areas of ability is a major key to having a more fulfilled and confident self-image.

Sometimes, people feel they have nothing special to offer, or think there is nothing unique about them at all. If you are not certain what you are best at, focus on discovering what your strengths are. Often, it's a short process, because our strengths are usually aligned with our passions, but we tend not to view those items as strengths.

I realized at a young age that I enjoyed meeting new people in any and all social settings. I think part of that is due to the fact that I'm genuinely fascinated by people's lives: their experiences, what they do, who they know, and what makes them excited or frustrated with life. As a kid growing up, the fact that my family moved around a lot forced me to get past the awkwardness and fear of new things and go into social settings with the attitude of making the best of it.

The next time you find yourself in a new setting, start by just observing the room or surroundings. Begin to get comfortable just being there. When you are as comfortable as you're going to get, make sure your zipper is up and just put yourself out there. Find someone in the drink line, someone standing next to you, the best-dressed or most shy-looking person—anybody you feel comfortable or interested in meeting— and say hello. Don't talk about the weather (*boring*). Be interesting and talk about something other than the weather or the hors d'oeuvres.

Although entering a room of strangers can be daunting, but it's really about asking questions and listening. Beyond that, it's about being genuine and seeing anyone and everyone as interesting at some level. When we look at someone as not being worth a few minutes of our time, then we need to do more than focus on our strengths— we need a serious realignment. You know yourself best, so depending on how strong you are socially can you determine where you can push that skill or work to develop it. You might decide to explore public speaking as a way to overcome your fear and share your expertise with others.

One of the best parts of having kids is being reintroduced to some of your childhood toys as an adult. At my house, we have thousands of Legos (which are magical to play with, except when it's dark and you step on them), but that's not my point. When you build with Legos, you can take any color and any shape and make whatever you want. Once you start, you are always building off of something that exists. As you build, you can expand, strengthen, or do both to create your Lego masterpiece.

Let's look at you as a Lego work in progress. You can take different colors and shapes and put them together to make something awesome. Each brick represents your passion, experience, goals, skills, funny laugh—all those things that make you uniquely you. As you picture yourself this way, you have to realize that we all have pieces that are various sizes and colors, and they all have different roles to play. Even the smallest pieces are incredibly important to making you who you are. If you lose that piece, or remove it, you may fall over or not look right. A strength is a strength, no matter how small you may think it is.

Making changes in your life doesn't require starting from scratch. Rather, build on some things that you are already good at. What is on that list? Which qualities are work-related and which are not? I'm positive you can take those skills and use them to expand your strengths into areas that you have been struggling with. Often, it just means coming at those areas from a position of strength versus weakness.

And speaking of weakness, another important factor about knowing your strengths is that it will help you identify your weaknesses more clearly. That's a good thing when it comes to hiring employees or looking for a new job. You will derive the most satisfaction by having a job that allows you to do what you are good at. This doesn't mean doing something that's necessarily easy. Without challenges we'd all be bored in five minutes or become perpetual resume writers. But be sure you are working in an environment where you can continue to develop the skills and talents most exciting to you. Knowing what you are not good at shows you the areas you have to develop, like it or not, and reveals what qualities in others you need to hire or delegate.

So, what are your strengths? Think about what you do naturally and well, and when you have your top five, be Lego-like and start building!

27

At a recent talk I gave, I focused on some of the points in *Life Kerning*. An attendee came up to me afterward and said, "I really enjoyed your talk, but you really didn't cover how to achieve balance in your life. How do you do that?" Without thinking, I simply said, "You don't."

I hadn't realized it myself up to that point, but this mythical "balance" is really a state of mind. That doesn't mean a balanced state is impossible, but it often doesn't play out as you see fit. Life never is equal or predictable in the long term, and it's up to you to be fluid and adjust. Talk shows, celebrity profiles, best-selling books, and the common commercial message all communicate that you can achieve the balance and the ideal life that you dream about—if you will only follow *their* advice. But in reality, true balance is all about your choices.

When I was a kid, I went through a stage where I wanted to read anything and everything I could get my hands on. I remember being addicted to the *Choose Your Own Adventure* books. I couldn't put them down. If you are not familiar with the *Choose Your Own Adventure* series, the setup went like this: You start reading a story, and eventually you come to a point where you have to make a decision about which option you think the hero of the story (you!) should choose. After you make your choice, you flip to that page to see whether your adventure will continue or whether you have just encountered an untimely end to your adventure. If so, you can go back and choose a different option.

I read these stories over and over until I could "perfect" my adventure as much as possible. I adored this interactive reading style, and it occurs to me that, in a way, we look at our careers and life the same way. We think that there is some perfect set of options, and if we just choose the right ones, our careers and lives will be grand. There is merit to making the right choices, but we all make mistakes, and, as you know, the future is unpredictable. The key is to realize this and take each scenario as it comes, simply for what it is, one day at a time.

Hopes, dreams, ambitions, and goals are all essential for your career.

However, understand that the timelines you set, the sacrifices you make, and the choices that fall in line with those will affect everything. How you manage all of it is really what forms a part of what we perceive as balance. The other part is a true understanding that there is more to life than work. Hobbies, friends, and other interests are essential to helping you feel more balanced. When you have more in your life than work, you feel less stressed, which helps everyone around you to be more productive, creative, and healthier in general. The correct ratio really comes down to each individual and his or her profession.

If you are feeling out of balance, review the collection of thoughts in this book and take a look at what you are doing outside of work. Do you have more than work going on for you? If

not, that's the first thing to examine.
The rest consists of aiming for a
balanced state that works for you and
encompasses what is important to you.

Maybe it won't be what you originally
thought, because you also want to
be a good spouse or parent. Or you
might realize that the time and sacrifice
required to become a partner in
your company or to earn 15 percent
more per year isn't worth it. That's
okay—again, life is too short to spend
it always working. But there is also
nothing wrong with loving your career
and wanting to work a lot. Having
a healthy ratio is what's important.
Here is the secret tip: True balance is
different for everybody (and it really
doesn't exist), but just knowing that is
half the battle.

DON'T BURN A BRIDGE

28

Don't you sometimes admire those people who can just tell someone to stick it? You know, the kind of person who can just turn and deal with a scenario then and there when they feel wronged. Instead, I'm often that guy who walks away and a few minutes later is kicking myself for not saying something.

I don't have an issue with an obvious grievance or injustice; I tend to handle those calmly and forcefully when necessary. But often I feel like I'm too much of a pushover. In hindsight, this has served me well on many occasions. There have been at least three times in my life when people I've dreamed about pushing off the side of a tall building have later ended up working with me and have become my friends. (There was also one occasion where my first instinct was right, and the tall building would have been the right decision.)

You never know how career paths will intermesh, reconnect, and evolve over time. This is even more likely if you work in a very specialized or narrow field. The people in your area of work will be the ones you'll have in your spectrum your entire career. This is important to remember, because many times, after you've gained some perspective, things that happen during a day or during a project aren't as bad as they at first seemed. If you can just process the scenario before you say anything you'll regret, there will be no need to wish for a time machine that would have tapped you on the shoulder to suggest that this was a great time to keep your mouth shut.

Often we feel wronged when something we believe, think, or want doesn't work out the way we had hoped. This is important to understand and think about before you shoot off a rude comment, angry e-mail, or some other nonretractable message. With the way we are all connected today, you can do great damage to your image and reputation by not thinking through how to handle certain difficult scenarios or relationships. Taking the high road can be difficult to do, but it's vital to develop some perspective. This is definitely one of those lessons that those who have been around the block a lot more than you can advise you on. Whenever you can, try to see the big picture.

When I get the urge to let someone have it, I often remember a trip I took to Europe. I was in the middle of the Louvre in Paris when I heard someone yelling my name. I turned around and saw a guy I played sports against in high school coming toward me. Toe to toe with me was a guy I respected but had wanted to beat so badly every time we stepped on the football field or basketball court against each other. We started catching up with each other lives over the past 10 years, and he told me a story he had heard through the grapevine about a falling-out I had had with one of our mutual acquaintances. As in most such cases, the story he'd heard was skewed and not completely true. I remember feeling bad about that rumor being out there, but I just smiled and said, "That wasn't how it really went down," and changed the subject. There was no reason to perpetuate the story or even try to change it; it didn't concern him. When I got home, I reached out to that friend, and we patched things up.

On the flip side, if you have been a jerk, there is a very simple way to diffuse the scenario: Say you're sorry and mean it. I believe those two words are becoming some of the most difficult to utter in the workplace today. People usually try to point a finger, make an excuse, or just deny the truth. Apologize and move on. If you are sincere, this means that, to the best of your ability, you will not again do whatever it was you apologized for. This hopefully isn't hard for you to do—and if it is, practice makes perfect. It's incredible how much better you feel when you make things right. And since you are not perfect, you'll probably have the opportunity to apologize sometime soon!

Not burning a bridge is often even more difficult when you are the boss. You might feel wronged by an employee whom you have done a lot for or have invested in through training or a promotion. It can feel good to let that person know how dumb you think his or her decision is, and sometimes you should share your perspective if you think it's a teaching moment. However, people do things based on what they perceive to be the best scenario for them. Tough love is sometimes the right answer, but so is handling something professionally. You never know—you may be working for that employee someday or, more likely, you may rehire the person because he or she had to see what else was out there to realize that working for you was a great gig.

HOW TO HANDLE A POTENTIAL BRIDGE-BURNING INCIDENT

1 *Take a breath. Try to create space to gain perspective.*

2 *Make a list of what you perceive to be the issues or annoyances. Reading this later will make you feel better, more determined; either way, you can look at a pattern and have a list of items to work with.*

3 *Address the source. Have a face-to-face conversation with the person. Be organized; have a list in your head; and stay calm.*

4 *When appropriate, have a witness on hand when you are confronting someone.*

5 *Killing someone with kindness is sometimes hard to do, but in the end, no one can fault you for simply being nice—and professional.*

In the end, you don't know where life is going to take you. Be honest. Don't compromise your values, but think before you spout off. Getting something off your chest may be best done by screaming in your car, going for a run, or indulging in some retail therapy—whatever works for you.

You never know how career
paths will intermesh, reconnect,
and evolve over time.

29

Our careers would be so much easier if there were a *For Dummies* book we could turn to for our position in our industry. And even though there are some fundamental life rules we all need to follow, the exact formula is elusive in the adventure of life. It's full of trial and error (probably more error than trial). Creating space to think about our careers is monumentally important. Being students of ourselves and the world around us helps guide our boat with as few sinkings as possible. We all take on water at times—and even need the occasional life preserver—but if you pay attention as you are sailing along, a lot of goodness can come to you. Making slight adjustments to your direction as you go is incredibly powerful and can help you navigate many disasters; it can completely change your destination.

When we become overwhelmed, depressed, or just sick of a situation, we tend to want to make *big* changes. Remember, those are *not* always the right decisions. Creating space and seeing what subtle adjustments you can make by adding, subtracting, and/or changing your perspective is a great habit to develop. As you write the headlines of your life, the question you should ask yourself is, "What story am I telling? Is my life story one I am enjoying?" Of course, you will have great highs and great lows. Drama, sadness, and joy—but is it interesting? Is it one that you want to be constantly adjusting and writing?

Take the time to *really* understand what makes you tick. Be honest about what your career desires are and how they affect your life goals. Take the time to put little tools and little moments into your day to help you manage what life throws at you. Create an ecosystem that helps you enjoy your day—one that you get great guidance from. May your attitude be one that helps you move on instead of sitting still. In the end, reading the story of your life should bring a smile to your face.

Take some time, and start life kerning.

It's your lucky day...there's more!

INDEX

ACKNOWLEDGMENTS

If I were truly able to thank all the people who made this book possible and all my various teachers, advisors, friends, collaborators, naysayers, discouragers, and influencers, it would be its own small book.

So, my thanks first to my mom for always encouraging me to draw and empowering me to go for it because no one was going to do it for me. Pops, I know you have my back, and I've got yours. Lynn, Dick and Beth thanks for the support and love. To Mr. H. for being an amazing teacher and creating the space to actually SEE me. To my Grandpa Ahrens for being at the level of awesome to still influence me some thirty years after he is gone.

Sarah, Mackenzie, Jackson, Quinn, and Ava, I love walking through life with you. You all are the most important parts of my day. You inspire me. I love you. Sarah, thank you for loving and supporting me all the time, especially when I'm a big knucklehead . . . which is probably daily. And for putting up with my endless ideas and mantras . . . I know I owe you foot rubs forever (it's now in writing).

To the design monkeys at Rule29, thanks for being a part of what we are trying to do and having faith in me. My door is always open. Kara (Cheech) thanks for being a part of this with me; I loved it all. You are amazing. Bob, your encouragement and help was just the energy I needed (since I do everything).

To Kevin, Brian, and Uncle Tony, I'm not sure where to start, except to say I'm a lucky guy. Todd, I know you just want to see your name . . . there it is, bro.

To little Justin . . . you are an amazing man. Thanks for helping change the way I see.

Claudia, thanks for being a constant encourager and helping me articulate my thoughts.

To all my clients past and present, thanks for choosing Rule29 with your business and allowing us the chance to collaborate with you.

To Dawn and Joe, thanks for putting up with me. I'm always here for you.

To Sean Adams, Noreen Morioka, and Terry Marks—thanks for the inspiration and brilliance.

To my amazing friend Larry and the team at Wiley, thank you! Especially Shannon for putting up with me, and Elana, Deborah, and Matt for taking a shot on a rookie.

And lastly to you, my readers. Thank you for picking up this book. If anything, I hope you realize that life is an incredible gift. Let's make the most of it by paying attention. Oh . . . and be awesome today.

29™

DID YOU LIKE THE BOOK? CHECK OUT WHERE I GET TO PLAY EVERYDAY:

RULE29
www.rule29.com
Our site where Creative Matter™ resides

RULE29 BLOGS
www.makingcreativematter.com
www.designersobriety.com
My company blogs about business, creativity and inspiration

TWITTER
@rule29
@justinahrens
@designsobriety

CONTACT
mail@rule29.com

ABOUT THE AUTHOR

Justin Ahrens' passion for life is rooted in his creative firm's commitment to "making creative matter™". For over 10 years now, Justin has led Rule29 in their commitment to great design and to helping others think differently about the world around them. Through a collaborative approach in both strategy and design, Rule29's culture is just as important as the work they produce. This is particularly evident by Rule29's involvement in numerous social causes, including their substantial work in Africa. Justin has also been a consistent voice for the design and business community as it relates to balancing life and career.

His obsession for design is only overshadowed by Justin's passion for being home with his wife Sarah and their four amazing kids (who think Dad's job is listening to music, drawing pictures, and playing on the computer).

Follow Justin on Twitter @justinahrens and @rule29.

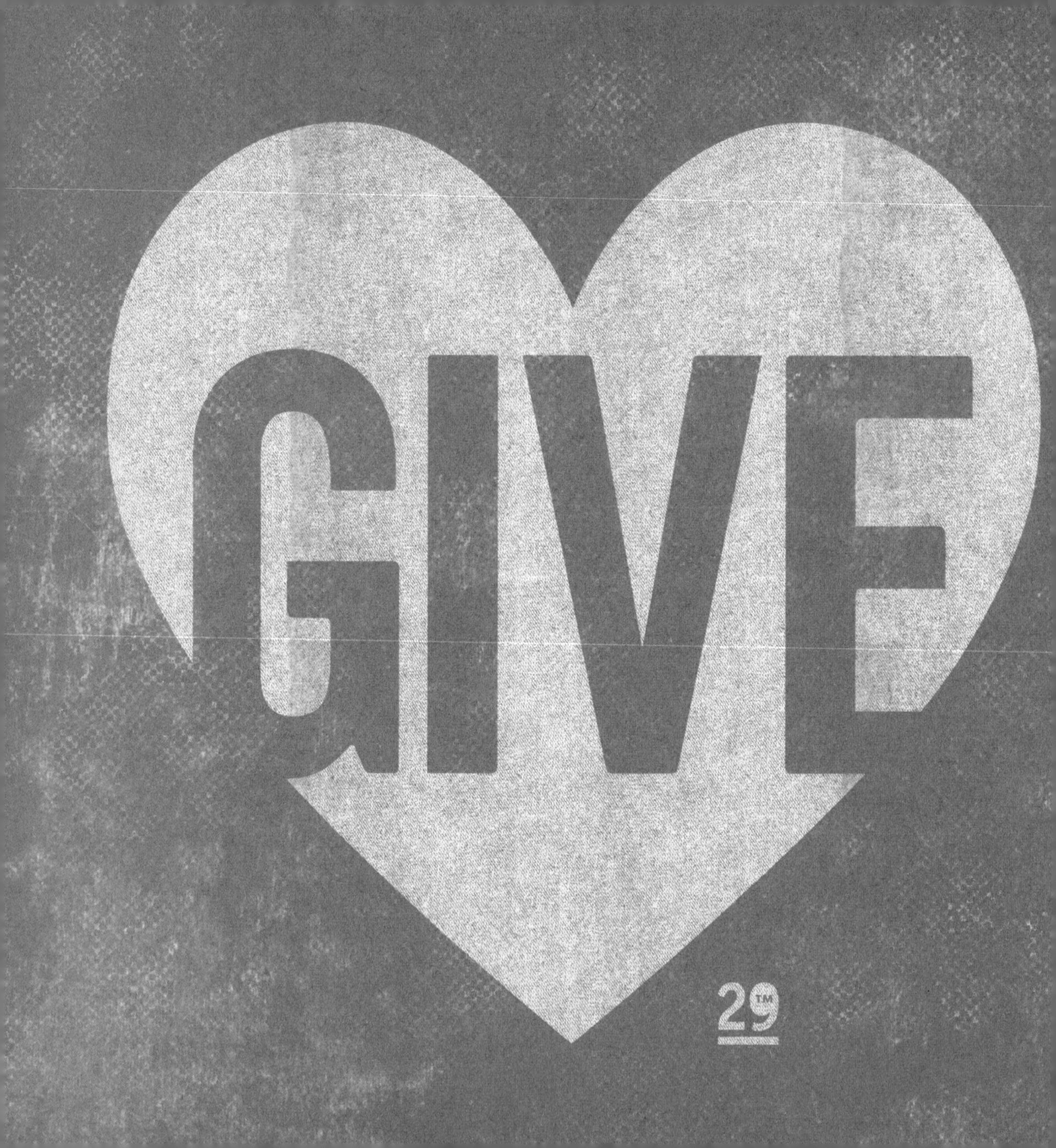
GIVE
29™

GIVE

The idea to give of oneself, or one's possessions, was never invented. It is an innate part of humanity. We give to share. We give to love. We give to make the world a better place.

Admittedly, it is easy for us to forget these simple realities midst the day-to-day chaos by which we have become accustom. The GIVE initiative was created in order for our team to be reminded of the joy (and responsibility) of giving. Starting five years ago, the Rule29 team has made a decision to give 20% of our time and resources to causes, ideas, and initiatives that we not only support, but enjoy participating alongside.

GIVE is simply a reflection of this collective.

We admit. We are not perfect regarding. There are plenty of others contributing to our world in more admirable ways. And we have learned from many of them. In fact, the more we pursue, the more we realize that giving does not take place in isolation, but in collaboration.

GIVE is about community. It's not Rule29's to keep, but to share. Join us as we give a little. Receive a little. And enjoy a lot. Perhaps this is just the Life Kerning you need?